Sex, Droogs, Music

Nowt But Madness Left

Part I

by

Paul Burton

Under the Auspices of
Burnt Hamster Publishing

To the Heady Heights
of
Rock & Roll
with a
Touch of Madness

Part One

A Debate With God

At the Mental Hospital, they made me very comfortable, fed me, kept me warm, and gave me a pleasant, quiet room to myself. The room had a firm but surprisingly easy to lie upon bed, with a single, thin, but surprisingly warm cover. The sheets were clean and the pillow smelt of fresh laundry. There was a spacious wardrobe, more than ample for my single garment, which was the dark blue towel-cloth robe I had escaped the house in and which on the right sleeve, held a map of the stars in spatters of white paint which had splashed onto me, into my hair, onto my face and onto that robe.

To any one else it just looked like a mess. Only "I" knew that the powers above had sent me a sign so that I could find their planet. All I needed now was a spaceship. I had been in the process of building one when the voices warned me of terrible danger and caused me to flee from the house.
It didn't taken long for the police to arrive. A semi-naked, part-painted gentlemen standing in the rain in the suburb of Sprotbrough will always attract an audience. My audience had stayed silent and invisible but the twitching curtains told me they were there so I just waited till the police came.

It took longer for them to convince me to go with them. I interviewed them in groups of three until I had winkled out the bad ones with trick questions and ambiguous answers. Coppers left when new ones arrived until after nine changes of personnel I was eventually left with three that I trusted and the voices said to go with them. By now though it wasn't a police car but an ambulance.

All through this, none of the men or women I interviewed would draw close to me. They stayed at arm's length, for they were unable to lay hands upon me. Nor could they command me. When I left with them, I left willingly and filled with expectation.

My arrival at the hospital caused a stir. My appearance itself might have been unremarkable. This was a psychiatric unit. They were used to strange sights. But the huge escort of uniforms was unusual, and patients and staff regarded me with wonder as I strode freely in at the centre of this crowd. A single voice from an invisible corner spoke out. "Look at the state of that!"

And then nothing, until I was seated in a secure room with twin WPC's, who tried to read my mind and gather my secrets. The corner was invisible because I did not have my glasses and at a distance of more than four feet could see no detail, only blurred shapes. I confused my thoughts for the WPC's by singing *"Bohemian Rhapsody"* aloud at full volume. I don't know if they understood the irony (*"is this the real life...is this just fantasy...caught in a landslide... no escape from reality..."*). One of them cried, though, so I dismissed her and another took her place. This time I sang Cat Steven's *"Father and Son"*.

Eventually, after more interviews, I reached a stage where I had found three staff who, I trusted, were on the right side and agreed to move into the room that I have previously described, and to wear the uniform green silk pyjamas which now covered me, as I hang my star map carefully in the closet.

After many questions and answers I had agreed *"for the good of all"* to take the pill they offered. This was after I had rejected my final choice of three, which was when I had noticed that the name badge of one man said not "Stan Vincent" but "Satan of Incest". I commanded him to leave in a most aggressive way, and he left to be replaced by "Dawn". I accepted her because I knew that the logo on her tee shirt was true. It said "Me? A Princess? Never!," and I knew that she would lead me to my queen.

The room was OK now. The bad guys had tried to trick me by placing on the bed a special cover which if it touched me would reveal my thoughts to them. It looked at first like an ordinary cover but when I focussed properly I could see the tell-tale signs of absolute symmetry that told me it was of alien construction... very high-tech. Once I had stormed enough for it to be changed I was happy and settled into the room.

There were strange lights in the room. A tiny red pinprick came from an indecipherable box on the wall whilst above the bed were two other pinpricks, one white and one red, which alternated in their flashing, in tune with my thoughts. At this stage, I accepted that having done all possible to maintain my security, I could relax. I knew the lights were there to probe my mind but decided that it was now time to let them in. I stripped naked, lay on the bed arms and legs outstretched and said *"Enter."*

The voice came immediately, it was one voice that spoke for many, yet the many were still one.

They thanked me.

The message was very simple. The time was here when the *Creators* were taking a look at their experiment and they did not like what they saw. War, poverty, oppression, cruelty, child abuse, domestic strife, and the advent of an order of chaos. These things were not new, but this species was now on the brink of a breakthrough which would allow them to leave the confinement of their own planet and reach toward the universe.

This was not desirable for *"the One"*, for *"All"* and a decision had been made to abandon the experiment, figuratively to scoop the contents of the petri-dish into the incinerator. However, the experiment had not been a total failure. They recognised that from nothing, they had created a life form which was similar enough to themselves to have developed the technological means to expand beyond its earthly confines.

This was a first.

The technology was important to them. They had also found an individual (*me*) with whom they were able to communicate. They wanted to take me, alone, away from the experiment, which they would then destroy. All I had to say was *yes* and the painless process would be under way. Give my consent and I would feel a tingling sensation and then wake up in a brightly lit lab surrounded by glowing beings in white coats. From me they would recreate a new and better version of the human race. All I had to do was to agree. I could already feel the tingling in my legs. I had been feeling it for weeks.

Feeling it and fighting it.

I said no.

Debate with God (Part Two)

He was amazed when I argued with him. At least, some of *Him* was.

I refer to him as "*He*", I can't help that even now. I was born a male and all my conditioning until then had been to think of God as male. *He* wasn't male. Nor was *He* female. Nor was *He* neither. Was *He* both then?

The truth is, *He* was many. *He* was all. Yet at the same time, the many things *He* was were "*one*". All this knowledge was a part of what had flowed into me when I had my "*magic vision*", as well as this instant ability to see, in my mind's eye, all that *He* saw, to feel what *He* felt, and though *He* tried to hide it from me, I felt   was amazed. At least that some of *Him* was. Some of *Him* was also peeved that I referred to *Him* as "*He*".

Some others of *Him* were less amazed and more sceptical. "I told you so," they said to the amazed ones. This animal is not ready to join *me*. It does not think. It merely reacts. It does not understand. But *I* did understand. It was God who did not and this amazed him.

"It is dangerous," said some. "It is wilful. If we accept it amongst us it will destroy our harmony and we will be sundered. This wilfulness will rise amongst our shared consciousness and it will become *Us*. It will become our God."

"Too late" replied others, "the link has been made and cannot be reversed. We could destroy this consciousness but we can never destroy our remembrance of *it* and of what might have been and the discord is already amongst *Us*. We must persevere. The cost of arriving at this point is too great for us to turn back now. To start again might lead no further. And is it not *our* God that we seek?"

"Then take it now!" argued more. "Bring it inside, nurture it amongst us, teach it all, that it may lose its wilful ways and become as we are"

I lay naked on the bed, as the red and white lights above flashed in rapid sequence on and off. It was like listening to a voice arguing with itself, which may .have been all that was happening. Maybe I was mad and arguing with myself. This must seem the most probable explanation to any reader. I was at the time confined by law under section three of the Mental Health Act. Nonetheless, the voices argued on without me playing a conscious role in the debate, and as they did, a very sane part of me thought "What a great idea for a science fiction story"

"See!" Cried a voice immediately. "All he thinks of is to write a book. He wants to use our gift for profit!" I relented quickly sensing imminent doom and promised there would be no book. I begged them please continue, they asked me once again to join them. I asked for their patience and further explanations and time to consider.

Chapter One

This line, the line of the prophets, was brought about by the creators interfering in their own experiment by introducing a strain of their own DNA into the species of man. They had done this by implanting the stuff onto meteors and allowing it to mingle with the existing life forms on our then primitive planet. The early results were men like Adam, Noah, Abraham, Isaac, Jacob and Joseph. After that the world became too civilised to easily believe in prophets, and the line became diffused. Its continuance depended on selective breeding which became difficult by the time the Pharaohs and their rising technology began to rule the world.

The skill was always strongest among the males, and by the time of Moses, the rulers had placed a ban on the rearing of any male children amongst the control group. Moses sneaked through by a fluke, and though he was the best of a bad lot, the creators used him the best they could, even though he was a mad man, and became a mass murderer in their name.

After Moses, who produced no reliable offspring, there were few who had the "*gift*" and miracles largely ceased. There were still purported miracles, but in fact they were tricks, sleight of hand, and the use of science disguised as acts of God, used to win battles, cross rivers, and destroy city walls.

Joshua dammed the river Jordan ten miles up but attributed its lack of flow at the borders of Jericho to God's intervention and the powers of the Arc of the Covenant. Then destroyed the city walls by undermining and explosives (which was not widely known) and claimed it was an act of God. It wasn't.

The line didn't completely die out though. There were still those who born with the DNA of the gods, could communicate, receive messages and sometimes perform amazing feats. But their influence waned as time and technology marched on.

There is an inverse relationship between the level of technology of a society and it's willingness to believe in miracles.

This didn't bother the creators too much at first. To *Them*, it was just an experiment that could be ended at any time. If it worked, great, if it didn't, they could scrap it all and try again. They might as well keep it going and see what turned up. Until the time of the Romans.

These guys were something special. They had organisational skills second to none, which allowed them to colonise large areas of the planet and make them their own, and a tendency toward developing technology for its own sake. This meant, in the eyes of the creators, that soon they would have the whole planet under one control, manage all the resources together, and develop ideas similar to their own, that might threaten them in time to come.

They weren't worried about Roman roads but about Roman space highways patrolled by Roman star ship troopers. So they intervened again.

They threw in one of their own. This time it was more than their DNA. It was an alien born on earth in a man's body. He came to teach ways of peace and good will to all, and he could work miracles and convince anybody. The Romans destroyed him and he died a horrible death, but not before he had gained enough strength of support to undermine the Roman principle of the world being built on slavery. I don't have to tell you his name.

His activities were enough to disrupt the Roman way, and after his passing the Roman idea grew weaker until they lost their empire, whilst his ideas grew throughout the world and democracy was born and practiced. He bred though, bred prolifically. The ancient stories of him hid this, but some modern writers have cast doubts on his celibacy and childlessness. And it is true. His offspring spread throughout the world and I am one of their descendants.

Yes, two thousand years later you are reading the words of a genuine descendant of Jesus Christ. There are many of us. Check out any psychiatric ward. But I am the first one who has inherited his abilities to fully talk to the gods and not go completely mad. That's why *They* chose me. I didn't go completely mad. Just half way there.

The Romans were halted, but the democracy that followed led to another great civilisation, the U.S.A. A civilisation that once again threatens to engulf the whole world with its power. The first of its kind since the Roman Empire. This time though it's more serious. These people have mastered the techniques of mass communication. Once their power is fully established it will be unbreakable and the whole resources of the planet will be united and channelled into one fund, which will be controlled by a people with the time and resources to look outward. They will find the gods and the gods don't want to be found yet.

They don't want to be found until they are assured that the people who find them have a truly peaceful and democratic base. They fear the Americans. Fear that this new species will seek to exploit the earth's resources for gaining power.

The gods had been looking seriously at stopping the experiment which at this stage they could easily do. They feared because there was no natural communication between themselves and those who were coming to power. Then they discovered me. Someone they could talk to, someone who understood. And they decided to give us another chance.

Discovering me was no accident. They'd been looking for me. They knew I was there. At least they knew somebody was. Maybe they had no choice but to once again pick the best of a bad bunch.

So why was I the best?

This is one of the things I asked the red light and these are the things *He* told me.

He told me my life story. I just closed my eyes and it was like a film playing. It took far less time to tell it to me than it will take for me to tell you so you will have to be patient. I have missed a lot out which is irrelevant but here's the rest.

This is why I was chosen.

This book is not an autobiography, nor is it about me, but there are some details of my life which are unusual and relevant. Mine is no ordinary life story. I have seen things and done things the average man has not and these things are parts of the reason I was chosen. Things you need to know.

This is what *They* showed me. I say "showed" because it was like watching a film.

Chapter 2

Before my son was born, I discovered that the woman I was sleeping with, the woman who eventually became his mother, had suffered severe childhood abuse.

Her personality resulted in her finding it impossible to trust. She was prone to drunkenness and unreasonable behaviour which included sudden acts of savage violence. I found myself in a situation where it became impossible for me to work properly in my career as an entertainments agent.

She refused to be left alone. If I tried to get out of bed in the morning to go to work she would pull me back and thinking this would be just for an extra half hour I would comply.

Half hours stretched into hours, hours into days and my office attendance was reduced to hurried forays to pay the staff, open the mail, bank the cheques, and stave off emergencies with soon to be broken promises of action.

When the brew of debts and cancelled contracts neared critical mass, I laid it on the line, and that's when the violence started. Before I reached the bedroom door there was a wildcat on my naked back digging its claws into my face.

Blinking away the blood I threw her onto the bed, and stepping over pizza cartons, I tried again for the door. No chance. Same again with extra peppers.

I am not a big man but am fit and trained in martial arts. For such as me, it is possible to remove a screaming, biting banshee from one's shoulders without hurting anything but feelings. I did this three times, losing skin and blood of my own but shedding none of hers. Striking no blows.

What is not possible is to turn one's back and open a door with the animal biting your ear and trying to blind you. Eventually I turned and faced *her*.

"I am leaving this room and will go downstairs. You will stay here."

I turned around. Repeat performance. Confronting it once more, I raised my hands and continued to speak.

"If you attack me again I'll be forced to hit you. Let me leave the room".

She flew at me. My left hand flicked out a jab (with the

right I can break small slates). The blow caught her cheekbone and I thought:

"Thank god it's over now."

No such luck.

Chapter 3

I come from a rough tough mining village.

I was educated at a faraway catholic grammar school. This meant that at six in the evening when I got off the train I must walk a gauntlet of hostile streets and alleyways to reach the sanctuary of home. Kids of twelve are a territorial breed and take unkindly to trespassers clad in green and gold uniform, complete with cap and tie, crossing their patch. It was only fair they should attack me. They didn't come into my "*bax*" either.

The *baxes* were what we called the tarmac strips that separated our identical rows of terraced houses, and they were sacred. Except for dark October teatime raids for bonfire wood, we kept out of each others' baxes.

I tried all ways to avoid conflict, varying my route to evade ambush, but by the time I was setting off from the railway station all the other kids had finished their tea and were out in force.

One alternative rout involved a dog-leg journey adding half a mile to the already long road home. This way bypassed enemy houses and ended in a convenient "*entry*" to my own bax, but it meant negotiating a steep hill over a patch of waste ground where the council was demolishing the old pit houses to make way for an exiting new estate. The only buildings left were a couple of deserted shops at the bottom of the street.

One day, I had reached these shops when I heard the warning sound of juvenile *swearing*. I immediately filled my pockets with "*bricks*" (throwable sized bits of broken house brick) and peered around the corner.

Two savages were mucking about in the rubble. It was Alan Nettleton and Steven Corny.

No problem: only two of 'em and neither were renowned fighters, Corny was only a bit bigger than me. Still I proceeded with caution. I wished myself invisible and set off at a pace that would put rapid distance between us but not give the impression of running away.

Never run from a pack. Nothing is more certain to result in a chase.

Of course, my green and gold stuck out like a beacon, they

spotted me, and the preliminaries began. "Cat-dog, cat-dog sittin' on a wall, eating cow-shit, penny a ball."

I was half way up, close to the fortress of my own bax, and I did not fear these boys. I responded with the appropriate formalities: "Proddi-dogs, proddi-dogs, sittin' on a gate." et cetera et cetera. (We had no idea of religious grievances; we just went to different schools.)

"Catholic bastard"

"Protestant cunts"

"Come over 'ere and say that"

"You come 'ere it's nearer"

The smaller one launched a brick.

Preloaded, mine were already in the air before his landed. He was throwing uphill, I was throwing down, and being experienced, I knew to throw high and many.

I launched brick after brick, not waiting for the first to land before getting two or three more into the air.

Their jeering turned to yelps of "shit" and "fuck" as my mortar landed round them.

A brick on the head could have caused serious damage but a foot away was as close as I got. Nonetheless they ducked for cover scuttling behind a three foot high broken wall. The demolition men must have knocked off early that day. Gleefully, I renewed my assault raising my elevation to bombard the wall in front and behind.

"You've fukkin' 'ad it now!"

Their strident tone was music.

"There's a big kid sitting behind 'ere and you've 'it 'im on the 'ed!"

My laughter at these lies turned to dismay.

What Phil Wren was doing behind that wall late that summer afternoon I will never know, but the undeniable fact of him rose up like Goliath.

Unlike Goliath, he did not fall dead; the stone I cast had raised but a terrible lump... and his wrath.

Get him!" he boomed, pointing the finger of vengeance.

It may have been "Get the bastard!" but I was not listening by now. Instead, I was legging it up the hill, but encumbered by a sack full of physics chemistry and biology (in those they actually gave you textbooks!) I had only reached the crest, when my fleeter footed pursuers drew level and grabbed me by the blazer.

Under other circumstances, I would have repaid this laying on of hands with a little laying on of my own. There would have been pushing and shoving and the pair of them would have ended on the floor. I have always had big legs and a low centre of gravity. In a push-and-shove, the other kid had to be a lot heavier than me or he came second. The chances of blows being struck were small and numbers didn't count because kids fought one-on-one in those days. But the big kid wasn't far behind and I stood and awaited my punishment as he lumbered up.

Fortunately, Wren was a decent sort. Guys who sit in the sun behind broken walls can't be all bad, I guess. His little men held onto me with wicked taunts until the puffing giant arrived. He gave me a lecture on the evils of stone-throwing, which I didn't hear, all my horrified attention being directed by his pointing finger to his lump, which got bigger with each throbbing pulse the more he ranted on.

Even then I defended myself verbally "They were throwing first and I di'nt know you were sat there."

Mr Wren didn't seem sure what to do, so he instructed his staff to throw my cap down an exposed abandoned cellar and I was released with a caution. Good old Phil. No doubt, he's a headmaster somewhere now.

This leniency stood the other two in good stead when I visited their bax to see them.

It was not just an ego thing, although ego was involved.

Peace of mind and sometimes your physical safety depended on reputation. They'd had hold of me, and to allow this to go unpunished meant I would become the target for the taunts of every kid in the village. Sure, there were bigger, harder kids than me around, but if you knew the streets, you could usually avoid them. The main problem came from the lesser hordes that would jeer from a distance but would keep physically clear unless backed up by a "big 'un".

If they sensed weakness though, they would close in.

Sorting out Necko and Corny was a chore that meant treading on dangerous ground, but it had to be done.

I put the word out that I was "after" them.

This meant that kids still small enough to be under the protection of parents, and who could safely cross from bax to bax at will, would spot the victim "*playing out*", and eager for the blood letting would run to find the hunter. Thus I eventually cornered each one alone.

I must have disappointed those jackals, because in the event, no blows were struck. No pushing, no shoving. Just a humiliating face down and the pecking order was restored.

Years later Necko and I became best friends. In my early twenties, I set up my own business and gave him a job, so the friendship ended.

I bumped into Corny again in my thirties.

He's a massive Harley-Davison-driving Hell's Angel!

We had coffee together and laughed about my old school cap. I guess you reap what you sow.

I could talk about other fights. Fights in which blows were struck.

Like the time when my brother and I were set upon at the bus stop by four of 'em, jealous of the fact that we'd pulled a couple of birds.

He took one blow, I dished out several and did a Bruce-Lee "*kata*" behind their car as it sped up the street with the occupants frantically trying to close the doors.

I was only a white belt then so the *kata* was faked; but nobody hits my brother!

The girls were impressed, but we left them and ran home laughing to relive it with Jim, who laughed with us till the dawn taboo. So proud was he.

I could mention the Brawl at Montgomery Hall.

We were gigging for the Youth club when a football gang got in and threatened the band. Big mistake. My brother was on that stage.

I had seen a problem developing from the minute these guys walked in. I'd told the youth leaders my concerns and they did their youth leader thing:

"You haven't come to cause any trouble now have you

boys?"

"Who? Us? As if we would." So we were left to get on with it.

There we were, five miles from home. These guys were on their own turf, there were a lot of them, and they were mostly a couple of years older than the audience. Under the ethics of the day, the kids watching the show were safe, but the lads in the band who were the aggressor's own age were fair targets.

Now the pack began gathering around the front of the stage making impossible requests.

"Play some Status Quo!"

"We don't know any mate."

"Oy cunt, play it fukkin' next or your dead, right?"

"We can't play it mate."

It was seconds before kick off and we stood to take a hammering to nil.   The only hope was to stop the fight before it started, so I started it.

Illogical? In terms of warfare, it was perfect logic. When the foe is superior and negotiation has failed; when you are sure that the onset of battle is inevitable; do not wait for the enemy to fire the first shot. Fire first.

This way, you fight on your own terms, you benefit from having the choice of battleground, and you have the element of surprise.

I pushed alone through the crowd, up to the front where the biggest was harassing Mick Robinson on guitar.   "What's up?" I asked, in my harshest tone. When faced by a hostile crowd always take on the biggest and never mince your words. Pre-punchup politeness does not pay. He wants to fight you, see? Or he wouldn't be there. And in front of his mates, he cannot let you off the hook. Also, he knows he can't lose so unless you wrong foot him it's just a matter of time before he backs you into a corner, and eventually, he will hit you.

Challenging with aggression puts the ball in your court. It puzzles him and makes him take time out to think what might be going on. His first instinct will be to look around for your "back-up" and to make sure his own is still there. When he does this, you need to act real quick because: It's like a development advantage in the game of chess. It's a good start but if you don't use it fast to create a winning tactic it will evaporate.

My tactic was to smack him in the mouth the second it opened. You might think that this would be the most likely thing to guarantee further hostilities but it is my experience that sometimes a preemptive strike can be the start and end of the whole conflict.

And if the conflict is already unavoidable, there's nothing to lose.

So I socked him.

Had it been possible I would have delivered a powerful lunge punch that would have taken him right out of the fight, and this might have been enough to sober his mates into conciliation.

As many as they were they may have still held back in fear.

I was facing some fifteen people, and would certainly have vanished without trace under a combined rush, but it takes an individual to start a rush, and seldom do any wish to front that charge against a proven puncher.

To deliver a lunge punch though, you have to adopt a wide legged stance at a distance of one long pace from the target, and you have to draw your striking hand a long way back in preparation. My situation did not allow for this so what he got was a sharp hook to the jaw from casual stance. Even so, it was enough to send him reeling backwards.

Magically, a space cleared around us.

This is where the logic of the kamikaze attack on the big one pays off again.

Had I gone for a smaller one, half a dozen others would have automatically jumped in to help him, and they would have quickly brought me down. But nobody jumps in to help the big lad. They wanna see him fight.

My hope from the start had been to take the battle away from the dark and noisy main hall, where anything could happen and no help would come, into the bright lights of the foyer, near the telephones, where the oblivious youth leaders were chatting each other up.

The big lad recovered and approached me within the circle. He squared up and accused me of necrophilia.

"You're fucking dead!"

He had no fear of the eventual result, but my earlier show of recklessness made him skirt warily. I faked a jab, dodged to the left, saw a gap in the crowd, and flew for the door.

They could easily have stopped me, but instead they darted aside, tripping over each other to get out of the way. If I was mad enough to crack the big lad, I might just be mad enough to go for all of them, and none of them wanted any. I made it half way across the dark disco floor before a rugby tackle brought me down.

Him again!

All he got for his troubles was another smack in the face as falling, I twisted to face him.   My hands were free whilst his were busy dragging me down, and I gave him a quick clean whack in the eye. Harmless but effective. He let go and I was on my feet and into the hallway in seconds.

I recall exactly what he said as we fell.

"Twice! Fucking twice! I can't believe it! Nobody cracks me twice!"

There was no pain or hurt in his tone. Just indignation and something like respect. It's a memory I fall back on when I need to smile.

Under the lights, I turned and took up defensive stance. This time my hand was poised for the lunge punch. The gang halted at bay, all in front of me now, a brick wall behind. I *kiai-ed* loudly, "Keey Aye!", gaining a second from their hesitation. It was enough. Within moments there was a bustle in their ranks and Steve Athey charged through, letting out his own *kiai*.

Steve was my best mate from school who used to drive the band's van to gigs. We'd done Karate training together and now he stood beside me and assumed the position.

Then came Robbo. Our fat guitarist.

I'd heard his instrument *kerrang* to the floor as the melee started and knew he wouldn't be far behind. Now he heaved his bulk into the clearing, red faced and sweaty. No oriental finesse here, just ham fists balled at his sides ready to mash the nearest nose.

The other band members, including my brother, stood clear, looking worried and sucking their fingers. We were still well outnumbered, but not even the big lad was prepared to risk being the first to enter that arena, and we held the ground until Mrs. Darwin, our "leader-in-charge", came onto the scene.

Sylvia calmed us down, and then, unbelievably, sent everyone back inside where the dance continued.

The band started to pack up the equipment as the DJ played on. We got ten minutes respite before they re-assessed our weakness and the first chair came flying up.

Suddenly bodies were climbing onto the stage to get at us and smash the gear.

I picked up a tubular piece of metal some five feet long, finished at one end with an oval metal ball for inserting the feet into for when we used it as a microphone stand.

Its potential secondary purpose had long been obvious to me, and at every gig I had always made sure that it was placed within easy reach, in case of need.

This may have been overkill.   Kill it would have been if the swinging ball had connected with anything organic. Fortunately the bobbing heads stayed back. They shouted inane comments but their owners kept out of my arc.

"Put that fukkin thing down ya bastard!"

"Come down 'ere ya cunt!"

Hard choice: Stay put and keep swinging, or dance with wolves?

They threw more chairs but the stage was high and chairs are hard to throw, and easy to dodge.

I swung, they hung.

Status Quo at last.

Sylvia did not reappear. She and her co-workers obviously realised it was just boys having fun, so I was left to it, until the Police came and escorted us home.

I could talk about the time Fat Gary, a business colleague, and a big bastard weighing in at eighteen stone, collared me (literally), outside the nightclub on Christmas Eve.

Gary had taken his business elsewhere, and then, to add injury to insult, he had ripped me off a few hundred quid. I had responded by sending him to Coventry.

At the time, I was running the entertainment in the town's main night club where I was allowed unlimited guests and an infinite bar tab. Before we fell out, Gary had enjoyed these privileges along with the company of the endless pretty girls that followed. Suddenly Gary was an outsider, a loner, and he didn't like it.

He had tried to "make friends" a few times but I wasn't having it.

"Go away Gary I don't wanna know you", was all I would say.

If I was with a crowd and Gary joined it, I would wander away, and the crowd would follow, leaving Gary by himself. After a while, this got too far up his nose and on Christmas Eve he decided to do something about it.

Earlier that evening he had tried for the umpteenth time to shake my hand, slurring on about bygones being bygones... season of goodwill, and all that. I was tempted. After all, the past is the past. But No! Even now Gary was screwing up Christmas present.

At the very time he was suing for peace, a venue which Gary's treachery had forced me to disappoint, was threatening to sue for a piece of me, and telling me to shove my agency up my arse.

I had fire in my guts and refused his hand, leaving him to drown his sorrows alone.

At the end of the night, myself, a little guy called Collo and two girlies left the club. The only other people left were the band and bar staff. Or so I thought.

There in the neon lit forecourt stood Gary. Right in my path. Ignoring his presence, I tried to walk past, but he put out a tree trunk of an arm.

"Excuse me Gary, we're going home now, would you move out of my way please?"

"Right we're gonna fucking sort this out!" His hand closed on my shirt front.

"Gary, let go of my shirt."

"Who do you think you fucking are?" he asked, gripping me harder and drooling.

I placed my left hand on his wrist my elbow up at forty five degrees, index finger and thumb pointing to the ground, ready for a maximum leverage twist into a painful lock. My hand only fitted half way around his fat limb. No grip, no lock.

It had to be a strike.

I put my Christmas-carrier on the floor and with my right foot, took a half step back, left knee bent slightly forward. I brought my closed right fist to my hip, my elbow bent out behind me. Forward leaning stance.

"Gary if you don't let go of my shirt right now I will put my fist right in the middle of your face."

"I'll fucking kill you, you cunt!"

One second, one step, three teeth, and half a lip later Gary's hand left my chest area taking my shirt buttons with it. Such is the power of the correctly delivered lunge punch. Only the wall behind kept him standing.

"That was your own fault Gary. I warned you and you wouldn't let go. You forced me to hit you."

Gary was spitting out teeth and muttering incomprehensibly. I stood there a while taking his bearings. He was still belligerent, still a threat.

The girls were shouting and the people from inside the club came running out.

"What's happened? What's happened?"

"Gary tried to stop me leaving. He grabbed the front of my shirt. I warned him to let go. He didn't, so I hit him."

"Fukkin 'ell!"

"Right, I'm going now." I picked up my carrier bag from beside me.

"I'm going to walk past you Gary and go to the taxi rank. Let me pass please".

He still blocked my exit and I had to move towards him to leave. As I passed him the huge man swung back his arm and brought it round with full force. My girlies squealed in fright.

I didn't even think. Just ducked low as he passed over me, carried forward by his own weight, and helped him on his way with a two handed shove powered by the momentum of my own rising, my right foot sliding ever so slightly into his path.

When you want to end a fight quickly, hit him with the biggest weapon you can find. The biggest weapon is always the floor, and it's always available.

Timber!

The ground hit him so hard he bounced.

Three times. I swear it.

Then he continued sliding along the concrete until his head stopped inches from a plate glass window.

Very lucky really.

Those windows are expensive to replace.

I have fought many times. Like I said, I could talk a lot about fighting, and this book is about a fight. But not that sort of fight.

So why have I told you all this? To explain myself. To explain that I hate fighting. I always have and always will. I fear it.   I do not fear pain but I fear humiliation, and so strong is that fear that I will avoid it at almost any cost.

The fights I have had have been forced upon me.

More than tales of battles, I could tell stories of the lengths I have gone to in order to avoid them. Stories of how I have allowed myself to appear cowardly and weak when I knew that this would satisfy the aggressor.

When I have had to fight, I have fought humanely and mercifully. The most harm ever inflicted by me on anybody is told of in the tale of Gary.

In such a situation, held at arms length by a very large, very drunk, very angry man with a grudge, what do you do? Could I have been gentler with him?

If I had given Gary jab or a slap instead of what he got, his anger would have increased, and with his capability undiminished, he would have mauled me like a bear.

Also, having landed my needfully powerful first strike, it would have been easy to have followed up with other blows before he could recover. Instead, I chose to walk away and risk further attack. Only training and fast reactions saved me from a hospital Christmas dinner.

I could have broken heads at Montgomery, or knocked spots off Necko and Corny back in the days of my youth, but there is no blood lust in me, no vengeance, no violence at all, except that which must arise from time to time because of the actions of others

and the need for self protection.
This is one of the reasons they chose me.

* * * * * * *

Also you never know when you might meet a huge man driving a Harley.

Chapter 4

Back in the bedroom things got worse. I could not escape. She would not quit. Time after time she attacked, time after time I fended her off. Each jab that landed was my prayer that it would be the last as I reached again for the door.

I tried to hold onto her instead of striking, but she twisted catlike in my arms, fighting against me with every limb tooth and claw. Being naked this was taking a high toll, and I was forced to fling her away onto the bed, from which she rebounded too fast for me to turn and flee.

Only when she was clearly exhausted but still came at me could I hold onto her writhing form.

"Enough. This has to stop now." I held her as she sobbed. Then I sat her down and told her I had to leave.

Before I got two yards she had scrambled through the fanlight and was outside on the ledge.

"Don't you dare leave me or I'll fucking jump."

It was only a single storey but the ground below was concrete and broken rocks. What I had witnessed that night made me believe she would do it.

I told her to come back inside and I would stay with her. Her five year old boy and one year old girl were asleep three houses away.

What choice did I have?

In the days that followed I was filled with wonder. I had always believed that the smallest act of violence between man and woman would immediately end any relationship. Instead she begged me to stay.

She said she felt a love so great that she couldn't bear the idea of parting. When I had wanted to leave the bedroom she had thought I was leaving forever, and she couldn't stand it. The hitting didn't matter to her. It was her own fault she said. She couldn't help herself she loved me so much. Our lovemaking was spectacular. I believed her and stayed.

I reasoned with myself that if we could survive such a terrible event we could survive anything. I felt that I had found a love that was true and filled with passion. I bought a big house and we moved in with the children.

I had hoped that the extra space would enable our happiness, and that the commitment I showed would calm her insecurities. Also I could now run the office from home.

I had lost contracts but by laying off the staff I kept my profit margins stable. This also solved the problem of leaving her alone, but it was still impossible to work.

She would not leave my side. She peered closely at anything I wrote and asked me to explain it. She listened in to all my phone calls then bombarded me with questions.

"Who was that?" "What did he want?" "Why did he say this that or the other?"

Sometimes the person at the other end of the line was female, and then the questions were worse. I had to be very careful how I spoke. These were faceless associates, but over the years I had cultivated chatty friendships. Now I found myself being brief and business-like to avoid a grilling.

Several times a day, she wanted to make love. She was a beautiful woman and I was a man so we ended up fucking all over the room with the papers strewn, the telephone ringing and the answering machine on overtime.

This looks great in the movies and it is a lot of fun. Until the work dries up and the bills come in. Especially the VAT bill. Value added tax!

The VAT Man is different from the Inland Revenue man. The Inland Revenue people are gentlemen to the core. You can delay your yearly tax returns and all you get is a friendly letter now and then. Most of the time they're not even after your money, just a few random numbers to complete the paperwork. With careful accounting and plenty of back pocket cash deals you can even get a weekly allowance. They don't even want to look at your books.

The VAT Man on the other hand is a bastard. He goes to the school of bastardology and gets the B.A.S.T.A.R.D. degree. (Without honour!).

That stands for Bullying Aggressive Sarcastic Twattish All-Round Dickhead.

Miss your three monthly VAT deadline by a day and the VAT Man sends you hate mail.   Letters with telephone numbers for amounts he "estimates" that you owe him!

"Estimates" is bastard-code for: think of a large number, add a couple of zeroes and demand it!

And they're written in blood!

Before you get around to opening these, he's at the front door with a face like a bulldog chewing a wasp, to "levy distress".

This procedure is well named. He distresses you by eyeing up your furniture and telling you he will sell it to pay his bill unless he gets the lot by four o'clock next day. The VAT Man takes it personally when you don't pay up.

I couldn't even find the VAT returns let alone complete them. They were probably used to wipe up something sticky after our ten times daily shagathons. I was three months down and daren't answer the door. I had to ask the woman to lay off me for a while.

I was diplomatic. Obviously I would rather spend time making love than doing work but she must understand that if the work wasn't done, I would go bust. Then I would have to get a "proper job" which would take me away from her more often.

She took this quite well. She only swore for half an hour. Most of it went over my head as it was in Italian but a rough translation goes like this:
"You and your fucking VAT, you love the fucking VAT Man more than you fucking love fucking me!"" You're a selfish ungrateful controlling bastard and, "you can keep you're fucking VAT I hate you!" and...

"I hope the Vat-Man fucks you up the fucking arse".

I've left out the more offensive parts.

Then she put on her clothes snatched a bundle of notes from my jacket and stormed out.   She would have sworn for longer but it was already eleven O'clock and the pubs were open.

Keeping the VAT was exactly what I had in mind. Hopefully without getting fucked up the arse. I settled down to work with coloured pens some blank receipts and a calculator. Some time later I was almost looking forward to Mister Bastard's visit, my masterful melange, now arranged in neat piles on the desk. Then I checked the clock.

Three A.M.

The kids at this time were staying with one of her ex's. He'd delivered them back in the evening and I'd fed them and put them to bed. With no interruption, I had worked solidly through to completion not noticing the time fly by. Only now did I concern myself where she might be.

Guilt hit me. I had let her out dressed like a hooker. An American hooker not a British one. The British ones wear track suit bottoms and anoraks and smell of stale cider. So they tell me.

She had been missing for sixteen hours. I knew that she would be drunk wherever she was, and I was fearfully imagining her dead in a ditch. I sat and watched the clock.

Four O'clock.

Four Thirty came.

Four Thirty One.

Four Thirty Two.

A year later, at four thirty three and thirteen seconds, I heard a diesel engine pull up by the gate. The clatter of falling coins, a drunken goodnight, the unsteady clack of heels, a key fumbling at the lock. She was home.

Relieved, I met her at the door with, "Where the hell have you been?"

"None of your fucking business you fucking asshole cunt. You don't want me near you, you and your precious office. I'll show you what I think of your fucking office."

First she ripped the phones out. Then; smash! Computer meets floorboards. I let her get on with it. It was only when she tore into my newly finished paperwork, ripping up my careful craftsmanship before my eyes, that I grabbed her from behind, holding her arms to her sides, "for Christ's sake stop it, the kids are asleep."

In response she started screaming.

"Go on, hit me you bastard, hit me like you did before. Hit me all you want I don't fucking care, I hate you, you bastard!"

I looked up to see a sleepy five year old at the door.

Somehow I calmed things down and got him back to bed.

"What's happening? Why's my mum shouting?"

"Don't worry son, it's just a dream, go back to sleep."

"O.K. Love you, g'night."

She slept the sleep of the dead while I paced the room until six, when the newsagents opened. Then I bought cello-tape and superglue.

Sleep was impossible so I spent the hours till breakfast time picking up the pieces. Then I got the kids back up and about their routines.

When she awoke at noon she wanted to make love. We hid behind the curtains when the knock came at the door.

This became a pattern for months. For variety she alternated between smashing up various household appliances, but usually it was my computer.

I asked the Social services for help but they were powerless. It didn't seem to matter to them that she wasn't caring for the kids properly. As long as somebody was caring for them, (meaning me), I was stuck up a shit tree. What about the violence?

They suggested I call the police.   The police couldn't help.   I'd called them one night before she got in. I told them I was expecting her soon and I knew there would be trouble. "Call us when it happens", was their advice. And, "why don't you try Social Services?"

I was helpless and she descended like a harpy, night after endless night.

I tried locking her out. She put her fist through the window and I had to call an ambulance for her lacerated arm. The ambulance men saw her pitiful whimpering blood-soaked figure and branded me vermin.

When she eventually came around after each night's binge, miraculously as fresh as new snow, I tried to reason with her. The first few times she was contrite and made promises. But soon she accused me of manipulation and control. When I contested this it led to new and worse arguments so I gave up and we had sex instead.

I gave up trying to reason with her that is. Not anything else.

I never give up.

* * * * * * *

The business was dying. I owed everybody. MThe building society wanted their house back and the VAT man was oiling up his tool. On paper I was finished but I still had cash in hand and I wasn't dead.

Most people would have gone under.
But there's another reason I was chosen.
I never say die.

Chapter 5

The debts were large but so was my turnover. A few months solid trading and a sob story to my next of kin and I could make a comeback. My next of kin was brother David. My senior by sixteen years.

* * * * * * *

David's suffering started when he was born.

Our wonderful but misguided mother wanted a priest in the family and for this, David was groomed. At twelve, he was uprooted from the village and delivered to the seminary in Durham. A boarding school for student clergymen.

A million miles from home.

Little David was pious to the core. His biggest transgression from faith was to say the rosary under his bedclothes by torchlight after lights out.

Told that he must keep up his morning and night prayers yet short of enough hours in the day to pray for all the people he knew, Dave devised a system.

Working with a handwritten list and his beads, he carefully reeled of an "Our Father" each for the important people in his life, Mam, Dad, and the Father Superior... and a Hail Mary apiece for lesser figures.

The glowing tent attracted the attention of Father Rusty McCann who walked the corridors at night to guard the innocents from themselves.   Spotting a rhythmic motion under the sheets he crept closer, fearing the worst.   He pulled back the covers to expose the praying boy.

David was gob-smacked when after explaining his system, he wasn't smacked in the gob, just told "Get to sleep boy" as Rusty handed back the list and made off grunting. It may have helped that he'd spotted a prayer allocated to himself.

The following morning at matins the minister gave the boys a stern warning on the evils of self abuse. David, who had no idea what this meant, was filled with curiosity which led to self discovery, and thus commenced his moral decline. He left the seminary before graduation, intent on finding a wife to reduce his need for sin and teaching religion to assuage the guilt.

He found the wife but not a life and years later became a recluse on a remote croft in the Hebrides. Before this he had played a fatherly role in my life.

At puberty I had risked eternal damnation by refusing Sunday mass. Our mother invoked David; to "get me back on the right track". I kept to my own track, but by eighteen years of age had read the bible...or had it read to me...cover to cover.

To Mam's dismay though, I wasn't convinced by the plot. I could see holes right through it.

Another reason I was chosen.

A quarter-century later I witnessed 9/11 live on T.V. I was moved to frustration. The tears I wept, less for the people burning, than for the aftermath I knew must follow. For the world my son must inherit. I raged.

I did not rage against Islam.

Had Osama woken up with a hangover and decided to get mean? I thought not. And those boys, the pride of their nation: Had they blindly followed the instructions of a madman, without considering that they were going to their own fiery graves?

No.

These people had a need and a purpose. A purpose so strong they would die for it. I wanted to know what was going on. I decided to find out and bought a Koran. That's when they really started to take interest.

But that is many years from now. On with the story.

* * * * * * *

The deadlines I had been given were only a few weeks away, but by now I had become expert at stalling people. I knew I could scrape through if only by a hair's breadth. Hair's breadths were my specialty.

Most things in life that I had enjoyed had come easily to me. I needed an adrenalin rush to make a real effort. And I had one now.   But to make the effort worthwhile I knew I had to get out of that relationship.

I got the loan, paid the worst of the bills and took the last of the cash to rent myself another place nearby. She came with me to look at it and decided she would move in there herself. I could stay in the house we had bought.

We had sex on the settee and my son was conceived.

Chapter 6

I must say a few things about the strangeness of that conception.

I was thirty five years old and childless. Considering the amount of unprotected sex I'd had in my life, this childlessness was freakish. I have had a lot of sex with a lot of women. We got a lot of sex through being a travelling band.

It worked like this:

Most of the gigs we played were in villages. Not town centres. We were strangers in a strange land and therefore exciting. Also we were guaranteed to be gone by morning, our bragging exploits confined to the van.

Girls who would make Charlie-From-The-Chip-Shop walk them home five times, before allowing as much as a good night kiss, would queue at the dressing room door for autographs. Often on their knickers!

This was nothing to do with morality. Nor is it that the local girls don't fancy the local lads. It was to do with gossip. Girls who do one-night-stands on their own doorstep are branded "slappers" by the time the post office opens the next day.

When our band played, the local Working Men's Club became the equivalent of a town nightclub, inhibitions fell and panties were dropped. But no sprogs.

We did it in the dressing rooms, on the stage after lock up and as often as possible back at the digs. You wouldn't behave this way today. But back then we didn't know about A.I.D.S. The worst we feared was a dose of the clap. And when that happened, you got it sorted out with one visit to the clinic.

The "tickle-in-the-pipe" was the worst of it. They could see at a glance you had gonorrhea. But instead of immediately prescribing penicillin they insisted on shoving something like a miniature umbrella down your Jap's-eye. It wasn't too bad going in but when they opened it up inside you and pulled it out again it made your eyes water. Then you got your shot and went home cured.

I don't think the tickle was part of the cure but if it was intended as a deterrent it didn't work. We were always back in the saddle fairly soon.

Crabs were also a hazard. Those buggers itch. The first time I got them I shaved off all my pubic hair, which itched worse than the crabs as it grew back.

Later I discovered Derbac Lotion, a single application of which got rid of the infestation in hours. I always kept some handy. Once bitten...

If we noticed any of the lads having a crafty scratch one of us would raise a knowing eyebrow and enquire, "Dere back?" To which the scratcher would raise a responding eyebrow and reply "Aye" and we'd pass over the communal bottle.

Speaking of eyebrows, our main scratcher, Steve "keyboards" Kendell once managed to get a single crab in one of his.   Not crabs, just crab.

For weeks we had noticed him picking away at what he took to be an itchy spot on his eyebrow. Eventually, he realised that this spot kept changing location and he got me to take a closer look.

There it was, grinning right back at me; the lone ranger!

Getting a crab in your eyebrows can be easily explained by a cunning linguist but Steve managed to go one better than that! He eventually got them in his armpit! Nowhere else on his body, just his eyebrow and his armpit! A very flexible man was Steve.

The other danger of sex was pregnancy but it wasn't something we worried about. A lot of girls were on the pill then, and they were happy to let you know it.

It wasn't something you discussed beforehand but as you approached the point of no return you dropped a subtle hint: "Can I come up you?" The usual reply was "It's O.K. I'm on the pill", or even "Yes, I'm 'due on'..." And if she said no there were always delicious alternatives.

.   So is this a book about sex?

No. Not specifically.

So why have I told you all of the above?

To explain how unlikely that conception was.

O.K. so I'd been having unprotected sex with his mother for months with no reliable contraception. They say withdrawal is risky but I've always had good control. The risk factor only made it more exciting for me. I always liked danger.

More reasons why I was chosen.

I feel certain that there are no unknown offspring of mine running around the world. If there were I would sense them when they were in trouble. It's in my breeding.

So, the first strange thing was that the conception occurred at all.

And the second ?

As I ejaculated I knew she would conceive a son. I felt it. I felt the moment of his arrival on earth.

Then I forgot about it, as the weeks that followed saw us drift apart.

Until...

Chapter 7

I see dead people.

Not with my eyes, with my mind. And not pictures. Not even voices, but I talk to them and I feel them as they were real. At least I used to. And that was before I went mad. Long before.

Spooky!

The first spooky incident was when I knew Jim was dying. He was three miles away calling from a hospital bed. And he wasn't using a telephone. A most amazing man.

Jim was my dad.

He was a coal miner, not trained in any other line of work, but he could mend broken watches. In those days watches were treasured goods. When they stopped working you didn't throw them away and buy a new one like you do today. You took them to Jim.

Ever tried opening a watch? Even with the right tools it verges on the impossible. Jim opened them with his bare fingers. He would peer at the insides from two or three different directions with just a twitch of his head. Then using a pin he would give a magic touch to some spring or cog and they started ticking.

He also made wonderful things out of salvaged wood. Several beautiful chess boards still remain in our family.

When I was ten he made a handle for my new saw, the backbone of my firewood business. The original handle was plastic. Working through the dark, he made a perfect job. A grained and polished replica of the ugly purple original.

I threw a tantrum when we found the old moulded handle was impossible to remove. "Useless. Useless!" Then I saw the blisters on his hands.

He could fix anything and never charged a penny. He just kept the old bits that occasionally had to be replaced, and saved them in the shed.

Washing machines, fridges tellies and ovens, he had lots of customers and we had lots of parts. Later he repaired even these and used them to create new machines. One day a fully functional electrically powered circular saw stood in our back yard.

The frame was made from roofing spars. The blade was the one item he had needed to purchase. It was mounted on an old pram axle, driven by belts from a Hoover, and powered by two separate washer motors. It could slice through spars in seconds and suddenly we could produce sticks faster than I could sell 'em. We expanded sales into the residential district and profits soared.

His secret was his amazing patience and eye for detail.

Ever get stuck trying to move a too large wardrobe through a too small door?

While the strong-men were heaving away with a square peg at a round hole, when they'd given up because it looked impossible, Jim would step forward.

Hand on his chin, tilting his head, he would tell them: "just get hold of it here....now here....back a bit...up..." and through it went as if it had shrunk. Some said he was a genius.

Greater than his patience with puzzles was his patience with me. I whined when the saw motors occasionally burnt out, and sulked whilst he fixed them again, but he never complained.

It wasn't the woodwork or the watches or even me that made him sick though. It was the pit. Jim worked on the coal face, where you breathed in dust for an eight hour shift five days a week. That kills you.

He had to quit the pit early, and although he was now mostly at home, he was never truly well. Always his chest bothered him. I'd become used to that, and the thought of him dying had not occurred to me.

There was a period when he was particularly unwell and every day when I got home from school he was in bed. Always I would go up to him and we would talk and play chess. We became very close. The love was big.

I was happy when he recovered sometimes and was up and about again. Each time he became bedridden I just thought he'd be ill for a while and get better.

By the time I was eighteen he was going to the hospital a lot for tests, and they sometimes kept him for a few days. That was O.K. Every time it happened they cured him. He was at the hospital, I was at work. All was well.

I was working at the Social Security office. At three in the afternoon whilst interviewing a benefits claimant I felt something. I knew straight away it was dad. He wanted me. I left the interview without a word, got my coat and left the office, without giving them any explanations, and rushed to the hospital.

I had to cross the town's busiest road. I did this without pausing, stepping between the fast moving cars like a bullfighter. I took the stairs three at a time and entered the ward where I had last seen him. His bed was empty. Then I saw Mam over to one side. They'd placed him behind a curtain to die in private.

I held my arm around his shoulders and said "Don't be scared dad". Mam said he wasn't.

He couldn't speak but I saw in his eyes he was glad I was there. Then it changed to concern. He had been resigned to die that day, but now he started to concentrate on pulling new breath through.

The nurse saw his struggle and brought him something in a glass. It smelled of whiskey. And something else as well.

He drank it, then let go.

We held him closely mam and me, counting his last harsh breaths, which went on long after he had gone. Only the nurse behind the curtain cried.

Thank you nurse..

The end.

It wasn't the end of course. It was the beginning.

I did not mourn straight away.

With the activities that followed the death, I was too busy, and it felt O.K... Like it was just some temporary setback... Everything would be sorted out soon... the visitors would stop arriving, we'd be finished with the endless cups of tea, and things would to get back to normal.

Then the permanency, (the permanency!) of death, hit me.

I'd gone into the kitchen to put the kettle on' getting out dad's cup as well as mine, and I suddenly realised he wasn't coming back. I found myself standing sobbing in the dark. I'm sobbing now as I write. It's wonderful.

I went to bed early so I could let my full grief explode. I bit my pillow so that I wouldn't make a noise. "Where are you dad?" And at the peak of my grief he came to me.

"Dad!"

"I'm right here son," he answered. And we chatted all night until the dawn taboo, parting only as the clouds opened in red lines of fire, lest Mam should catch us not getting our sleep.

There were no voices, no sounds, and the logical explanation is that I was just thinking to myself. Nothing more.

But it was more.

I entered a state of mind in which all of it was real. The things we talked about were not one sided versions of my own opinions, but definite two way traffic. We disagreed here and there. Sometimes he gave me advice, which I sometimes took.

It was real, and it happened often.

A similar thing happened when Mam passed on.

She had not been unwell, just tired and some headaches. I was a full time music manager now for my brother's band. One morning I was arranging a gig when he phoned to say that Mam had suffered a minor stroke. She was unconscious in hospital where they were waiting for her to wake up. They expected her to recover.

I knew immediately she would die that day.

I also knew that it wasn't going to be for a while yet. I knew she would wait until I came. My live-in girlfriend was away at work with the car, not due back till tea time. The hospital was miles away. I took in the news, checked the clock and carried on with my work.

At five pm Elaine came home. I explained the situation and we left for the Hospital.

My brothers were chatting quietly a few yards from the bed. Mam was lying on her side, her regular breathing audible through a tube. The nurse explained that she could wake up at anytime. Most people did in this situation. All we could do was wait. I was left alone with my mother.

I took her hand and whispered. "I'm here . You can go if you want."

Nothing. Just the sound of her breathing. I matched the rhythm with my own. We were breathing together.
in...out...in...out...in...out. I slowed my breath a beat.
Out.......in........ out.......in..........out. Mam's breathing slowed with

me.

I stopped. She stopped. The heart monitor went flat and gave out a faint tone.
The nurses didn't notice, nor did the brothers. There was an ice cream van in the distance playing "Green-sleeves". I watched as the melody floated skyward.

Then I panicked and called the nurses, and Mam's poor body was whisked off to another room, where they tried to raise a few more breaths. But she was away, riding the sun crossed clouds.

I don't know why I performed that ritual. I hadn't thought anything about what I was going to do when I got there. I'd never heard of anything like it. But I knew she would leave soon after I arrived and I did what I felt was right. It just seemed to have happened by instinct. I didn't kill her, nor hasten her death in any way. But I just knew with certainty that before departing she would wait for me to arrive, and with all the brothers present to say their goodbyes, she could leave in peace. I didn't cause the event , I just had a certain foreknowledge of it which seemed instinctive.
Which of course it was.

It came as no surprise when Mam started to join my regular chats with Dad. They were often there, in my thoughts, sometimes together, sometimes separately, I could always tell the difference. It was like an open three way phone line.
Usually I'd call them up to give me advice on some pressing worry, but other times it would just be to say hello.

* * * * * *

When I first met my son's mother, before I slept with her, I knew she would be trouble. She was more of a gangster's moll than a businessman's companion. She was hanging about with the local Mafioso bouncers who ran the doors of the town's nightclubs, and presided over petty drug trade. She was not the sort to take home to Mother. But I asked Mam about her.
"Mam." I said. "Will this girl be suitable for me? Will she make the right mother for my son?"

I had always known I would have one son and that he would be just like me. But it was not on my mind. It was a distant destiny which I accepted and took for granted. When I asked my dead mother this question, about a girl I had known for a week, the thought had previously been absent from my head.

Mam said, "I can't help you with this one son, you're on your own," and I was delighted. I let out a whoop and sprinted the last half mile of my jog, back to where the woman was waiting. Later that day we made love for the first time.

I had put this from my mind by the time I rented the new house, but in that moment, when we had sex on the settee I felt something.

It was the moment that he came to be.

Then I put the thought away and went on with the routine of daily life. You might question how it can be possible to forget such drama.

The answer is that at the time these things happen, you know something's going on, but you don't understand what it is that you're feeling.   Later you rationalise and find logical explanations.

Later still you realise there are none.

The serious notion I had felt in the moment of ejaculation was dismissed, and over the next few weeks we saw little of each other.

I had more or less gotten over the relationship and was going about my business. I was returning from the bank, when all of a sudden a "presence" came into me. It was Mam.

This was unusual in itself. All previous conversations had been initiated by me. Now here she was knocking on my brain, demanding admittance.

The road I was driving was very narrow with hairpin turns. When I enter these states to chat to my dead relatives, everything else stops. The car carried on and my body kept driving it, but I was elsewhere.

"Hello Mam" I said grinning, tears forming as usual, hairs prickling my scalp. "What do you want?"

"You've got to keep that baby!" Immediate response. "He

is very important."

"What baby?" Startled.

In my mind I saw a picture of an infant, still wet from his mother's loins. Dark hair, face screwed up in a post birth frown, yet a face I recognised him as unmistakeably mine. This vision continued until I became aware that the car, without my help, had successfully negotiated the bends and was now moving along the straight carriageway that led to my office.

I did a quick detour. Ten minutes later I was at my ex's house. She had just returned from an appointment with family planning clinic. I did not know this when I walked in. She had not intended to tell me she was with child. "You're pregnant aren't you?" was my opening comment. She was convinced that the woman who advised her at the clinic had tipped me off.

What made this seem more likely was that this woman was Maureen, the estranged wife of my brother David. Although they had never met before, it was quickly obvious to Maureen who this client was, and who the father must be: David had described her to his ex; she had an unusual name and she was distinctly Latin looking. Not a hard deduction in a small town.

Maureen sussed her straight away saying "the father is David's brother isn't he?"

The professional had advised abortion. The woman spurned had thrown in a few insults to my family name. Even so it was easier for the mother to believe that her confidentiality had been betrayed than the story of the conversation I had just had with my dead mother.

Nonetheless we kept the child and brought him up together for three long years before we managed to find separate lives.

It seems that some things are simply meant to be.

And now that I have explained these things about myself I must take you back to that room I was in with the strange flashing lights, for you need to know what was going on.

Chapter 8

Outside in the corridor, the nursing assistant hurried about his rounds, checking on all of the new patients, who were automatically put on twenty minute observations. He made his observations by lifting the small curtain on the window of the door. That's why the curtains were placed on the outside of the rooms. So the nurses could do their "obs". A quick peek at the patient in room six had told him that this one was lying safely on the bed, and he noted this on his clip board as he moved rapidly around the rooms. Only ten minutes till tea break.

The rooms were old fashioned in design. Big and clinical with high ceilings and high windows of which only the top parts opened. The hospital couldn't risk giving potentially suicidal psychotics access to windows that they could open themselves, or they would be climbing out.

The beds were firm foam mattresses covered by a polythene protector under the sheet. This was in case of accidents. Much easier to get the urine off polythene than out of a mattress. The polythene had breathing holes at regular intervals so that air could get in and out when the patients got on or off the bed. Otherwise there was a danger of bursting the sheet with compressed air. The moving air caused a hiss whenever the mattress was compressed or released. The hospital staff didn't notice this. They never gave it a thought. It never occurred to them that strange unexplained noises might add to the paranoia of an already delusional mind.

They didn't know about the air currents either. Being a hospital it was important to avoid draughts so all the doors were virtually air tight. The whole ward was a kind of vast air-lock. Sometimes windows around the ward were opened on purpose to let in fresh air. This caused an air current which meant that when the doors of the observation rooms were opened the current might cause the fanlight windows to open and close with a bang, as if of their own accord. This was no problem though. Unless you were a patient suffering from paranoid delusions.

Each room was fitted with smoke detectors on the ceiling and temperature censors near the light switch on the wall. These had little red and white flashing lights that were always flickering on and off. Nobody on the staff gave this a thought. It never occurred to them that these lights could be interpreted as signals from aliens.

Nor did it occur to them that it might not be the best thing for a paranoid delusional patient to be immediately confined in close proximity to a large group of others suffering similarly.

I was hospitalised because I had run semi-naked out of my house fearing an invasion of the body snatchers, and the first thing they did was put me in this strange room with these strange doors windows, and flashing lights, and people peeping inexplicably in at me from the outside every twenty minutes.

There was another strange thing about my room too. Noises; weird scratching noises, that clearly came from one or other corner of the room, when my eyes told me there was nothing there. The room was four stories up and its outer window faced onto a large courtyard, closed on three sides by the identical tall buildings of the hospital, and on the fourth side by a high wooden fence. Patients were sometimes allowed out into this courtyard to smoke or get fresh air, so it had to be sealed off from the outside. The result was an acoustic trick, and the sound of a pigeon scratching on the gravel floor was funnelled straight up and magnified, coming in through my window and echoing back. It sounded like someone or something was in the room with me, but whatever it was it was invisible. More confirmation to me that something very strange but very real was going on.

Later, when I became well, I rationalised it all. The lights were various sensors, the window opened and closed because of air currents, the curtains which were strangely situated on the outside of the door, twitched every twenty minutes because I was being observed for my own safety. The sounds were echoes from the courtyard below. I didn't know any of this at first though. To me, the strangeness of it all was all evidence of the alien conspiracy I was already convinced of.

I didn't know what was really going on. But I knew that I had experienced strange events, and these new things were not the strangest. They were nothing compared to the disappearance of my son and his family from their home.

After I discovered they were gone, which I did by visiting

the house in a fit of desperation at one in the morning, barefoot in the rain, I had decided I could no longer ignore the signs. From that moment I started to believe that all of this was a supernatural occurrence. By the time I was in hospital, I was expecting strangeness.

I was in alone that room for seven days, except for occasional visits from staff to bring me meals and make up the bed. That's the standard time for new patients to be in isolation on twenty minute "obs". I just settled in and prepared my defences in case there was a battle.

Each morning and evening they also came to give me my "meds". Ten mg. of Olanzapine twice a day. It's an antipsychotic. It also makes you very sleepy and restores your appetite.

My appetite was restored, and each time they brought me a menu from which I could choose a meal, I enjoyed the luxury of picking out everything I wanted. Everything was delicious and there was plenty of it. Whoever had captured me, they were sparing no expense to ensure my comfort. Suddenly I was eating regularly after weeks of starving alone in my house before I ran.

There were numbers and strange symbols on the menus though, and I couldn't understand them. A helpful nursing assistant explained to me that this was a code.

That was the worst thing he could have done. I took it to mean that the people who were sending the food were trying to communicate with me, send me a message of some sort, and expecting a message back.

It also told me that this particular nursing assistant (he was a staff nurse actually), who's name was Jim Buck, was on my side. He was working inside the organisation, trying to help me.

I took his information on board in the strictest confidence, and tried for a long time without success to crack the code.

It was a simple enough code in reality. It just gave information about the relative properties of the items on the menu. Orange juice was coded "A" meaning it was low fat, chips were coded "C" for high fat content. That kind of thing. It was to help patients select the meals best suited to them. In my malnourished case it was obviously best to select items coded as "extra nourishing." I was looking for something deeper though. Some information about what was going on.

The fact that the people who were sending me food were trying to communicate with me in code, and this had been explained by an inside agent, all fuelled my fantasy, that, although I was trapped here inside this room, other agencies were at work trying to help me. I didn't say anything though, except to tap the side of my nose in a gesture of confidentiality to Jim, thanking him for telling me about the code.

Jim acknowledged my gesture in the usual way, and pretended to hurry on about his business, as if the communication with me hadn't happened. I understood. He had to maintain his "cover".

Jim Buck. Jim Buck? I had seen his name on his badge. I had had to peer very closely because I didn't have my glasses. I also had to be careful in making out the words, because written words at that time with me tended to morph unexpectedly into other shapes. Like the first day I was brought in and had studied all the nurses and their names very closely, before deciding which one's I would allow to be with me.

I had settled on "Dawn" because that was the name of the *blonde*'s best friend, and somehow I felt that she might be tied up in these events. In fact, I felt as if I was being put through a series of tests which if successfully passed would lead me to her. I thought that having reached "Dawn," who's T shirt read "Me, a Princess? Never!" and was therefore a clue, it would soon be led to my queen.

The other man present with Dawn was a male orderly whose badge read "Stan Vincent". I had given him a crucial examination and had accepted him, but something was nagging at me. Something wasn't right. I looked closer at Stan's badge, and this time the words morphed into "Satan of incest!" I thrust him violently away and tried to warn Dawn, who he had obviously fooled. Stan tried to come back toward me, but I held my ground and threatened him with my fist. I knew I had seen through him, even though no one else had, and it was now necessary to be as extreme in my behaviour as it took, to get rid of him.

I was obeyed by the hospital staff. They took Satan away and replaced him with another person, who passed my scrutiny. To me this was more evidence of my power, of my authority amongst them. Obviously to them, I'd just flipped my lid. They didn't know it said Satan on poor Stan's badge.

Then they showed me my room, room 6. Another clue. 666, the number of the beast. A number that had mysteriously appeared on a recent supermarket receipt. Six pounds sixty six. I knew it was another sign, but whether I was the beast myself, or merely an important watcher looking out for him, I couldn't say yet. I would have to figure this out later, but meanwhile I made them change the bed cover, because the pattern was too symmetrical, and was obviously of alien construct. They hurried to obey, and I accepted the room and the power they gave me.

They were just glad to get me into the room, into the bed and out of the way. They would have told me anything I wanted to hear to achieve this, even if it meant letting me believe Stan was the devil and the bedspread was evil.

Jim Buck? I peered at his badge. Then it hit me. Jim Bu. An abbreviation of my fathers name "Jim Burton". My father had been dead for years, but now he was sending me messages and clues from the afterlife. I was to trust this man. He might even be my father in person, in a different body.

It was because of this trust that I asked Jim Buck many questions, and when he had time within his busy rounds he tried his best to answer them. I explained to him that everything I saw in newspapers or on television, seemed to have personal significance to me. Jim explained that I was hyper associating and drew me a diagram of the human brain to explain. He drew pictures of the frontal lobe and the hypothalamus, with arrows going back and forth, and he explained how the signals between them were getting mixed up, and that this was because of a hormone imbalance my body had developed. I was impressed. This Jim was clearly a creature of great knowledge and distinction among his kind.

The rational mind left in me wondered if these weird experiences could be linked to the drugs I had taken. The drug taking had started when I was with the *blonde*, which had only been a short while ago. I hadn't touched drugs before I met her. I needed to think about this but first I had to get out of the relationship I was in. The one with the *Alien princess*.

Chapter 9

After my son's birth she lost interest in me. I did all the things a good man should do, and more. I worked hard, provided well and tolerated her excesses, which resumed just a few weeks after the birth.

For two years, I worked at my screen and phone with his cradle by my side, while she drank the town dry, soaking up my earnings faster than I could make them.

If I hid the cash she would borrow from my friends, for me to repay later.

When I stopped this scam she started to pawn our goods. I would find out about the latest transaction every four days when we had our twice weekly new start.

Always I hoped that each time would be the last and I allowed myself to be convinced by the sex that accompanied these reconciliations. Always I had to bite into the sour apple of failure and try again.

After two years there were few goods left to pawn and I had to put my foot down. She spent two hours calling me awful names.

"You're a pathetic little wanker."

"You're scum."

"You're an asshole"

"Everybody says so, nobody likes you. You stink"

Our baby was sleeping beside her on the settee. At least, I thought he was asleep. Then a puzzled little voice piped up, "I like you dad".

Hearing this she got up as if to leave the room, ashamed I thought, but as she passed my chair she stabbed me in the face with a tin opener.

I went to the hospital.

Afterwards, I walked long roads looking for answers in the silent street lamps that glinted from the fallen rain. I thought of leaving, going to the law, but I knew that in front of a court she would perform like an abused angel. It would be hard to convince them to place the child with me. I would get visiting rights but mostly he would be in her household, helpless and alone.

And who would his new daddy be?

I shuddered to think.

What if she took him back to Germany where she had been born? What then?

I screamed at a passing lamp-post, daring it to complain lest I smash it with my fist. No answer.

"My God" I thought, "I'm cracking up". A new surge of desperation hit me and I called aloud to the sky, "Mam, Dad, God, help me here!" The answer came down, a faint echo in the falling mist, "I can't help you with this one son, you're on your own."

I had to get out. My body and my heart were aching, my pride was smashed, and now that the anaesthetic was wearing off the stitches were tightening in my face.

I wanted to lie down and die.

But there are some fights you can not quit.

I went back.

When she awoke she kissed my wound and we made love all that afternoon. At times it seemed like a test. Which of course it was.

Chapter 10

I'm a chess player you know. Jim taught me.

It seemed a slow game at first. Something I did on rainy afternoons when the fields were closed and the dog unwilling. We had a small wooden set in a case that opened out as the board.

One day I was bored and left to my own devices. There was no daytime television then and no computer games, so I got out the chess. Jim had showed me how you could play against yourself and I gave it a try.

It was dull. But later on when the set was put away I couldn't lose the mental image of the black queen sweeping up the board leaving devastation in its wake, and the next day I got out the set again. Pretty soon I was playing every day.

When I improved, Jim and I often played late into the night when there was no school in the morning. I thought I'd soon mastered him but I see now that it was a trick.

Trickery has a bad press. Tricksters are bad guys. Unless they're called Jesus. That guy used tricks all the time to teach things to people.

Jim was letting me win. Letting me get a feel for the game. That's how you teach children complicated things. Through tricks. Maybe that's how you teach everybody. Maybe that's what this book is about.

When I was twelve, my teacher, Brother Joachim, taught us the names of chess moves in Spanish. This led to me starting a chess club which Steve Athey and I ran together.

More than the chess, we were interested in collecting member's subscriptions. We these found useful for tuck shop funds but we liked the games as well.

We also got subsidies from the school for entertaining away teams at our home venue. Money for drinks and food for the guests. We ate well, fed them well and made a profit.

Through a freak I won the third year championship. It was more a fiddle than a freak. We played a Swiss-Tournament system in which each player played every other player twice. Two points for a win one for a draw. There were thirty kids in the contest. Not all of them managed to fit in all of the games and by the end of the term we each had several left to play.

The masters stated that the player with the most points at close of season would be the winner regardless of games not played.

I had selected my opponents carefully, avoiding the strong, picking on the weak, winning mostly by the four move checkmate. I was standing at third or fourth in the table with enough games left to play to win outright.

I spent a mad three days cajoling unwilling patzers into playing me at break-times and I built up my points to joint second place.

John Blythe was leading. He was two points ahead. I had only one scheduled match left against Sean Fury, a no hoper who had been absent for weeks. The next break, when no one was looking I entered up my two points against him on the chart on the classroom wall.

No one noticed my fraud and it was declared a tie between Blythe and me. The champion was to be decided over one last game after school on the penultimate day of term.

It was fair to take the points against Fury. If he had been there I'd have played him. If I'd played him I would have won. I settled down that afternoon to play the big match.

We progressed to middle game with no advantage either way. Then I made a blunder and lost a piece. It was my move. I didn't know what to do so I just sat there not moving.

We used no clocks for those games. They were played to the end however long it took and they usually didn't take long. But I could take forever if I wanted and Blythe couldn't do a thing about it.

After half an hour he got up and said he had to go for his bus. I was the winner. My bus had left long ago but that was fine. I won.

Some would call it cheating. I call it improvisation. There are few boundaries I will not cross to get what I believe I deserve. Exactly the kind of person *they* wanted for the job.

* * * * * * *

I got a tin medal and a round of applause in class the next day and Brother Wilfred, the headmaster, paid us a special visit to congratulate the winner.

When he realised who the champion was, he generously

said how surprised he was to find me spending my time on something worthwhile for a change. What he meant was it made a change from whacking my backside with his cane. He used to do that a lot for no reason at all.

One morning, I'd just arrived at the school when Wilf stormed in and ordered us all into the hall. He lined up twenty of us, and went down the row administering six-of-the-best on each pair of buttocks.

I discovered afterwards that before my arrival he had cautioned the occupants of the room for making too much noise, and when the noise continued he had decided to administer a painful solution rather than give a second warning.

No appeals were permitted so I just stood there and took a whacked arse, not even aware of the nature of my crime.

On another occasion, my class was waiting for old Reg Varney, the lame art teacher to arrive. In his absence I had been pretending to pick the store cupboard lock with a paper clip so that we could get out the paints and start the lesson.

Usually you knew when Varney was approaching the room. There was a strip of window at about five feet high along the classroom wall looking out on the corridor. This meant that you could see the heads of the tallest teachers as they passed. Varney was too short for you to be able to see his full head, but you could tell it was him by the way his bald patch bobbed in and out of sight with each step he took. He had a terrible limp from being shot in the war. How we used to curse those short sighted Germans!

I didn't think I was doing anything terrible by joking with the lock. I couldn't have picked it if there was a million pounds in the cupboard. I never thought it could be taken seriously. I was just having fun. Nonetheless, I was watching the window, so I wouldn't be caught out of my seat.

But Varney tricked me.

The cunning bastard had synchronised his limp so that as I looked up, he bobbed down and I didn't see him until he was framed in the doorway, glaring at my paperclip jiggling in the cupboard door. Obviously he thought I was about to ransack the contents and indulge myself in an orgy of colour.

I was sent straight to Wilf.

Explanations were futile. All Wilf wanted to know was

would I bend over please and away he went. Whack! Whack! Whack! Six more of the best.

They don't call it that for nothing either. Those holy men really gave it their all when whacking butts. One teacher, Doctor Burdett, actually took a run up before his strike, when he been awarded that day's duty.

From these experiences I learned three things:
Firstly, the "system" was unfair. If the little guy was caught in transgression, real or imaginary, he would pay the price.
Secondly, the system could be beaten. You just needed enough cheek and a willingness to accept the consequences if you were caught.
Thirdly, history only care about winners. Not their methods. My name remains in the school yearbook as the original De La Salle Chess Champion. John Blythe, who was a much better player than me, is forgotten. My apologies John, if we ever meet again I will give you this medal.

I also learned how to play chess and how to speak Spanish.

* * * * * * *

Chess is a lot like life.

When you are a beginner, you're happy only with blazing attacks, whether they produce triumph or disaster.

When you have gained experience you start to recognise that games aren't won by blinding flashes of skill but by slowly building up one small advantage after another, usually having to risk giving away some other small advantage to the opponent as you build on your own strengths.

Later I became a very good chess player. That's another reason they chose me. But when I returned to the house that dismal night I was still a beginner at the game of life and was planning my blinding attack.

I was planning murder.

Chapter 11

I didn't plan the murder for selfish reasons.

My own peace of mind could have been achieved by walking away from the situation. I would have felt guilty about leaving the mother and her two children but I felt I had done everything I could to make things work and that I couldn't succeed only because she was impossible. Leaving my son with her was different. I couldn't leave him to that fate.

What else could I do? Stay and brave it out? Play the gentle husband role, doing all I could to divert her attacks toward myself? Could I raise him in that atmosphere and expect him to stand any chance of becoming a well balanced adult?

I thought not.

I could see him ending up in psychiatric care by the time he was eighteen.

Would I stand any chance in court of gaining custody? Very unlikely. The courts always tended to keep a child with the mother wherever possible. And even if I succeeded, I would be bringing him up alone, without brothers or sisters.

What kind of life would that be? What kind of life would he have with his mother alone? A terrible life I thought. I couldn't see it any other way.

I had often got excited when she stayed out particularly late. The later it got the more chance someone had strangled her in an alley. When she got home the relief was always mingled with disappointment. And always, she came home... Eventually.

If only she would die. My life would become free, I could keep the two older children and do them a favour by bringing them up properly and I would have ready made companions for my own son.

Also I would benefit from a fifty seven thousand pound insurance policy designed to pay off the mortgage in the event of an accident. I could certainly use that money, especially bringing up three kids on my own. But I was concerned that this might lead to a more thorough investigation than I would otherwise face, if she died mysteriously, without financial gain to myself. I thought long and hard about my method.

Break her neck and throw her down the stairs making it look like an accident?

My ju-jitsu training meant that I knew how to snap a person's neck quickly and cleanly. In theory. Of course, I'd never put it into practice and I wasn't one hundred per cent certain of the result.

Also it might leave tell tale bruises, or the fatal injury might not prove to be consistent with her fall. No good. My plan had to be completely without flaws. I had to make certain I wasn't caught. There was no way could I bring up my son from a jail cell.

A fall from a higher place then?

There was a viaduct a few miles from where we lived. A picturesque beauty spot, with a view over the whole Dearne Valley, from a height of thousands of feet. Could I persuade her to take a walk there with me?

Maybe.

But what if she struggled as I tried to push her off? Raked my face with her nails? Could I explain away a struggle? Perhaps we argued and even fought. Then she fell or even jumped.

But what if someone invisible to me was watching?

A peeping Tom perhaps, or a concealed dog walker, or even a far off observer with binoculars. Or what if the fall, as high as it was, didn't kill her outright? I couldn't be certain of any of these things so I abandoned the idea. But the thought of a fight gave me more ideas.

How about if, in the throes of a passionate argument she attacked me with a knife? After all, she had stabbed me with a tin-opener once.

But the tin-opener incident was undocumented. I had called the police but had told them I had been assaulted in the subway by two men. I later received a thousand pounds compensation from the criminal injuries compensation board for the scar it left. And it would only be my word. Worse, it might provide extra motive for murder if I mentioned the tin opener.

Another thing: What if a single stab wound didn't kill her? I had seen a crime series on television, which told me that accidental death from stabbing was only given as a verdict if the victim died from a single wound. One stab is an accident. Two stabs is murder. If I stabbed her and she lived I was fucked. The plan was no good. I ditched it.

A ditch!

That was it!

My fantasy was that she wouldn't return home one night but would be found dead in a ditch, murdered by some unknown assailant, picked on because she was a scantily dressed female walking alone. What if I followed her one night and became that assailant, returning home later, never to have been out at all?

But what if I were seen? Got bloodstains on my clothes? How would I alibi myself? No. It couldn't be done. Not with the watertight guarantee I needed. I was back to the drawing board.

I settled for suffocation.

The pattern was, that when she came home drunk, once she had verbally assaulted me for an hour or so, she inevitably fell into a coma that lasted two hours. In those two hours she was as if dead. I could lift her up; carry her from room to room: attempt to make love to her every orifice (occasionally succeeding when I overcame my erection problem), and no way would she awaken, no matter how rough I was.

I did these things considering it to be fair play. If a beautiful naked woman was going to sleep in my bed thus preventing any other naked woman from fulfilling that role, she was mine for the taking, so yes, I fucked her in her sleep, and she didn't notice.

How much easier would it be to slip a plastic bag over her head and wait till she stopped breathing? In the morning I would call the ambulance. I'd gone to sleep next to her woken to find her dead in bed. The coroner would find a ridiculous amount of alcohol in her blood, (I once counted forty-two Budweiser's in one day and night), and conclude the obvious. She'd drunk herself to death. I prepared my materials and waited for her to get back.

Sure enough off she went into dream-land. She was sat on the landing, her back to the wall where she had collapsed. She was breathing through her nose. I pinched her nostrils together to test the effect. She didn't breathe for a while, but she heaved a little, although she didn't wake up. Then she choked and her mouth opened gulping in air. I put the bag over her head securing it with a thin elastic band that wouldn't leave a mark.

Then I waited

For a long time nothing seemed to be happening. She kept breathing inside the bag, slow and regular. How long would it take?

It took too long.

While I was watching her through the cellophane, I thought of the children in the next room. Could I really live as their father, witnessing them grow up wishing they had a mother? Knowing I had done this to them?

I took off the bag and went to bed to brave it out.

In the morning we made love.

I wasn't a killer.

Another reason why *they* chose me.

Chapter 12

I didn't escape from her until she finally met another man she fell in love with.

I had persuaded her to go to college. She started enthusiastically but soon novelty wore off and she was reluctant to attend.

Her departures from the house were bliss. I was able to catch up on work and the finances recovered. When she stopped going I suffered again for months, but then she developed a new interest.

Suddenly, she was up every morning at eight, dressed and waiting for the bus, not coming home till the college closed at 5 P.M. I still had all three children to care for, but I got more work done than I would with her hanging around. I could sense that something was wrong, but I was happy enough.

She started to stay out later and later, eventually staying out the whole night. At this stage I had to ask questions and she was honest enough to admit that she was seeing a guy who was on her course. Andy.

I told her that this was fine by me. Now that there were no longer any secrets they could meet in the open. Would she mind staying in during the daytime to keep the kids off my back? She could now date the guy in the evenings like normal people do.

She was panicked into a rage by this suggestion. Her reaction told me something else was wrong here. The guy must be married!

I had friends on the college staff. It took a lot of calls but I am tenacious. I finally pinpointed the guy in a far off village and rang the number. A woman answered.

His wife I thought!

It turned out to be his mother, and after establishing that he had left for college, and was unmarried, I thanked her and said that I would call him back later. She was too wise for this ploy. She knew something was amiss and probed me with questions.

O.K. I thought...what's the problem?

I explained that he was sleeping the woman I was living with. That this was OK, as I wanted her to leave me, and now she was sleeping with Andy, she probably would. I had just checked to make sure he was unmarried and available, that's all.

She was upset. No way would her son do such a thing. He had a perfectly good girlfriend right there who was all but a member of the family.

"No problem," I said. I had every confidence that his new conquest would see the girlfriend off, whoever she was. My own experience told me how alluring she can be when she wants a man. The other woman didn't stand a chance.

The lady was not having it. She would sort it out right away! She would speak to her son, get him to send the newcomer packing, back to me and her children.
Eek!

Patiently, I thanked her for her concern and told her that she didn't need to sort out a thing. I was happy that my ex partner had found someone else and I wished the new couple well. I had only called to avoid the possibility of a "household with children" being disturbed. Finding the man to be free and single, I had no objections to the relationship continuing. Meanwhile, my relationship was over and I was glad of it.

Still the lady was insistent, and I had to plead the case that any disturbance from her at this stage would cause disruptions to my own "household with children," before she agreed to keep quiet, but for a few days only!

I went to my son's mother and told her what I had done.

She went ballistic.

I calmed her.

All she had to do was tell the guy that everything was out in the open. He could dump the girl at home and start officially seeing whoever he wanted. The mother would get over it and we could all move on.

Off she went to do it. She returned in a state.

Andy had cursed her, cursed me, cursed my dog my cat and my budgie and left in a huff. And I didn't even have a budgie.

Fair enough, I thought, back to square one.

I could have happily accepted her leaving me for another man if it meant she left my life, but I could not stomach the idea of some guy with a happy home life, including girlfriend in tow, getting a bit of spare at my expense, whilst I played baby-sitter at home.

If the guy had decided to cut-and-run, then, so far so good. I was only bringing forward the inevitable. He seemed to have done just that and I felt I had achieved something. She was miserable in the house for days, but so what?

Meanwhile I used the opportunity to pursue my own ambitions with the *blonde*.

Chapter 13

I first saw her across a crowded room.

Tom Morton had organised me an invite to the prestigious *Carcroft Club*. The *Carcroft Club* was the biggest live entertainment venue in the district. It staged live bands two nights a week and sundry artistes almost every other night. The club had used a rival agency to book their shows but had been disappointed lately.

This was insider knowledge which only people like Tom, who had ears everywhere, were aware of. Tom was an insider because he owned his own club, *Morton's*.

I had met Tom many years earlier at the start of my career with my brother's band. After a seemingly chance introduction, Tom opened door after door for me, asking nothing in return. At that time he was president of the *Rugby Club*, and manager of the *Civic Theatre*, so he had contacts. When he bought his own club he gave me free office space on the second floor. I became the agent for his entertainment, and my bands were allowed to use the club for rehearsals through the daylight hours.

This meant I spent a lot of time in his club. I got to know his barmaids well. Especially Theresa.

Theresa was a slightly too voluptuous redhead who fell in love with me at first sight. She was married with an infant, but her marriage was on the rocks and we had wild times together before the *alien princess* came along. One night the *princess* walked into the club as Malpas' girlfriend and walked out as mine.

Malpas was Neil Malpas, head bouncer, ex-heavyweight boxer, and drug baron.

I was fearless and very self assured, but Malpas was a professional hard man with a reputation to uphold. The conversion of my princess could have been very rough for me, but Tom knew even bigger bouncers.

Tom knew Martin Kamara. Six feet six in his socks. A reputed killer. And Tom knew where the bodies were buried, as well as holding the key to free all night drinking sessions at his club.

There had been a supermarket robbery in Doncaster. Two

masked men broke into the house of the manager early one morning.

They made the manager phone his secretary and then tied him up and put him in the boot of a car. When she arrived they showed him to her. They also showed her a shotgun, and told her what would happen if she didn't get all the cash from the safe and deliver it to them in the car park.

They got away with the money, but sometime later Kamara was arrested on suspicion and they put him into an identity parade.

There was a problem. Where do you find a dozen six-feet-six black men to stand in line? They solved the problem by finding some very tall white men and blacking them up. Except for their hands. They looked like the black and white minstrels. But with white hands.

The papers got hold of the story and made it a laughing stock. Kamara walked away Scot free. Not that he did it of course. Martin Kamara was a gentleman.

But you didn't mess with him. No sir.

So, the *princess* walked away with me and Theresa was dismissed.

Years later I was with the *princess* at *Carcroft Club*, on Tom's introduction, and in walked the *blonde*. When the *princess* and I had been happy I never felt like looking at other women. When we became unhappy I simply dared not look at them.

But I looked at the *blonde*.

The *princess* saw the look but instead of her favourite trick of emptying her pint of beer over my head she told me to go for it. So I did.

What really happened was more complicated.

"That's what you fucking need" she said, "Something young like that with blond hair and big tits."   "Why don't you get her and let me get out of this fucking club, I hate it here, I hate you, you're horrible."

I denied my desires of course but I knew she was right.

Now, persuading her to go became a necessity, and eventually I managed it. I dropped her off in town and returned to *Carcroft*, but the *blonde* was gone.

In this event, I was relieved, as despite the *princess's*

disinterested attitude, I knew she would kick off at the idea of me showing a real interest elsewhere.

I returned home at midnight and waited in for the *princess* till dawn. But the idea of the *blonde* plagued me.

In the weeks that followed I re-visited that club several times and managed to sight her twice. Each time I placed myself discreetly in a seat I knew she must pass on her way to and from the bar, watching her, timing her journeys, trying to catch her eye.

Zero response.

Whilst this was happening, the *princess* and I were constantly arguing. She was still staying out late, and coming home to cause a scene… and usually sex in the mornings.

Only after I had released the *princess* to her new lover did I have any success with the *blonde*.

In hindsight it seems I am committed to being a one woman man, whether I want to be or not. Almost as though someone was watching over me and dictating my strokes of fortune.

Which of course *they* were.

Chapter 14

Let me tell you about table soccer. In America they call it foosball. I mean the sort they play in English pubs. The tables have chrome rotating bars which are manipulated via plastic handles through a flick of the wrist. Brighouse tables.

You can see a similar table everyday in the American sitcom, *Friends*, in Joey's apartment, but that one is a clumsy imitation of the true Brighouse table. It compares only as a rough terrier compares to a pedigree greyhound. Even if Joey and Chandler were experts, which they are not, they would not be able to make the ball do tricks there, as you can on a Brighouse table.

I became an expert when I was very young.

At age eleven, the joint Christmas present for my younger brother and me was a small version of a Brighouse table.

That dawn our parents awoke to the clattering sound of spinning bars and shooting marbles as he and I fought out the F.A. Cup Final on the landing, just outside their bedroom door.

Never was a Christmas gift used more. We played it every day for years, until it eventually fell to pieces under the strain.

Later, at sixteen years old, I got my first taste of a full size table at the *Red Lion Pub* in Conisborough. I was working at the crisp factory through the school holidays along with a couple of older university students. Every college has a Brighouse table in the bar and every male student develops some skills at the game.

By the time I was sacked for throwing spuds, I had discovered a whole new dimension to table soccer.

Returning to sixth form I enlisted my comrade, Steve Athey, into thrice weekly afternoon outings, using the chess club profits as our finances. We found the *Wapentake Pub* which had two tables, and we set about becoming true masters of the craft.

In this we were encouraged by a weekly television programme called "The Indoor League". Here they showed pub sports of the day, including darts, bar billiards, and of course, my own favourite, table football.

They ran national competitions that included teams from London and Scotland, but the finalists for three years running were a team called Kopax and Bowkett, two men from the town where I live. It was exciting to see people from our home town on television.

It inspired us. If they could do it so could we, and although the sport died out as the more profitable space invaders machines took over the local bars, we pursued Kopax and Bowkett from pub to pub, always missing them by a whisker.

In the thrill of the chase I acquired the true table soccer skill which witnessed by the naked eye look like old fashioned magic. I became so good that I could make the ball disappear.

I don't believe in magic. Never have and never will. But Arthur C. Clarke once said that any sufficiently advanced science is indistinguishable from magic and I believe in that.

One second, the gob-stopper sized white plastic sphere was motionless at the feet of my player. The next it was gone. A sharp sighted spectator might spot a blur of motion, but most people only heard the "thunk" as my ball vanished time and time again into the opponent's goal. It looked like magic but it was science. A mental calculation of the size of the ball, the gaps it had to pass through to reach its destination, and a physical effort in the flick of the wrist, all combined. Thunk! The ball was gone.

Some people can play for years and never develop this skill. Others acquire it in a matter of weeks. But none master it like I did.

It's a hand-to-eye coordination thing. It turned out that I had this in spades. Something to do with the way I was created.

I also have a strong will to win. Which has something to do with why I was *chosen*.

* * * * * * *

Eventually I found Bowkett in a pub. First name Frank. We played and he won. But he cheated and I knew I was the master. I proved this when I met him many times over the following years.

He wasn't even particularly good at the game, but he turned out to be a good conversationalist and we became friends.

* * * * * * *

The *princess* moved out to live with Andy. She married

him, had his child, and seemed to settle down.

     I had my son every school holidays and weekend. Mondays to Thursdays I was free to work and play. Life was sweet and I had my blonde

     The minute I became single I had set out in hot pursuit of her.

Chapter 15

Sitting alone in a darkened room all day does things to your mind. The longer you have to brood about your problems, the deeper you look for solutions.

When you have a problem solving mind, it makes it worse, you struggle harder. A non-stop dialogue goes on all the time. It seems like there's someone else talking to you, except, you know, it's your own internal voice. At least at first you do.

I got so that the *voice* became a constant companion. I could transpose its personality into whomever I imagined myself talking to. It could be my brothers, the doctor, the social security or the police. It was as if they were there in the room with me holding up their own end of the conversation.

You could liken this to playing against yourself at chess, moving the pieces on both sides of the board, trying to make yourself forget the plans you just made as white, when you take the black pieces and then looking only at attacking the white pieces on the other side.

The *voice* is more realistic than chess though. In one-man-chess, no matter what you do as white, it's impossible to completely forget what you had in mind when you switch to black. All such games are doomed to mediocrity. You always know what the "other guy" is thinking.

With the voice in the head it's different. *It* develops a life of their own.

When they asked me at the hospital if I had been hearing voices I truthfully answered no. My ears had picked up no sounds. But I can understand how people with a lesser sense of reality say that they heard "voices."

I recall the time I first held one of these conversations out loud. I was alone in the bedroom, picking skunk. I'd found three bin liners full of stems in evil Kieran's waste bin.

When you grow skunk, you wait till the buds grow big and then uproot the whole plant. You hang it up to dry for a few days then pick off all the big ones. If you've got plenty of time you can pick off the smaller buds too but if there are a lot of stems to pick they often get discarded with the small bits left on.

Kieran had a lot of stems.

Kieran was my next door neighbour. By day, he was a motor mechanic, fixing small faults on people's cars and creating bigger faults as he did so, to be sure that the customers would be back next week for further repairs. That was his honest side.

By night he grew skunk in huge quantities in a converted back bedroom. He had all the equipment. Huge sun lamps which consumed vast amounts of electricity but ran for free from his doctored meter, and a complex system of irrigation pumps that circulated water through lots of trays of extra rich compost in which grew his plants.

He would nurture fifty seedlings per crop and these took twelve weeks to reach maturity. Once picked, they would be replaced immediately with a new batch. Each harvest would net him something over ten thousand pounds, and this was just what he grew at home. He owned four more houses. On paper these were "development properties". "Houses" he had bought to renovate and sell or lease out. In reality they were skunk factories.

After I left the *blonde* and moved back into my own house, I had become friendly with evil Kieran. He soon pointed out the financial potential of my empty garage.

Foolishly, I gave him the go ahead and within a week he had installed thermal insulation (to keep the plants warm and defy infra red detection from police helicopters) and another fifty plants were growing in there.

The deal was to have been fifty-fifty, netting me over five grand, but something went wrong with the crop after he had picked it and my share turned out to be some scraps of weed. This may have been because I upset him with an attack of conscience, sparked by an incident involving my son and some older youths.

I had employed three thirteen-year-olds to clear my large back garden and cut back the overgrown hedges. They were a street-wise trio who quickly recognised the smell emanating from the garage. They joked about it with me before getting on with the job I was paying them for. My son was fine with this and at first got on well with the older boys. He was a tall nine-year-old then.

I had given him money for sweets and retired to the bedroom to smoke some of Kieran's product whilst I contemplated my woes, leaving him to help in the garden.

They stole his sweets. I was awakened to cries of "Dad, Dad! They've hit me. Sort 'em out dad".

I rushed out at a stroll to see what was wrong.

He had fallen foul of the three when they demanded an unfair share of his candy. When he objected they pushed him away and took the whole bag.

Knowing he had my support, the boy had manfully launched in to recover the goods and he had been punched. He fought back against the leader but was quickly defeated and had come to me for justice.

Out I went.

I told the lads to down tools and fuck off without pay. "That's a nice smell" said one. Pointing at the garage.

I was fucked.

I paid them off at triple the rate and they went. I then relented at my foray into dealership and told evil Kieran the problem...

He was furious and decided to take the crop out immediately, together with the irrigation system and lamps, removing all evidence that could get us fourteen years in jail. The crop was ripe but after harvesting and selling, evil Kieran told me it had been premature so I got no money.

I knew evil Kieran was ripping me off but I was powerless. I couldn't exactly go to the police about it. So I retaliated in other ways, and stole things from him. Taking bags of discarded stems from his bin wasn't really stealing, but it gave me satisfaction to profit from off his laziness... and there I was, picking skunk. Three bags full, ten plants per bag.

I'd been at this a couple of hours and had produced a fair quantity into a washing up bowl at my feet as I sat on the bed. My hands were covered in a green film of dust as I picked. As I carried out the monotonous task I let my mind wander wherever it would go.

Without realising it was happening, I went into a trance-like state, where I was holding a conversation out loud with the group of teenagers I had suffered the misfortune of getting to know some weeks earlier.

* * * * * * *

I'd bought a goat.

Thirty five quid out of the paper and there it was eating the brambles that had choked my quarter-acre garden and defied my mower. A few weeks later, the goat had trimmed the hedges and given me a turf like Wembley stadium.

So what it once ate my underpants. A small price to pay! It was a fun animal. Occasionally I would let it roam the smaller front garden in view of passing school kids.   That was a mistake.

Deprived of the company of my own young son, I found myself looking forward to school opening and closing times when crowds of children would gather at my gate, hoping to see the goat. I sat there, with goat, and enjoyed seeing the children. I chatted to them and their parents, never realising for an instant that this made me look like a pervert.

I had my son's Labrador pup and a pet rat too. Between the four of us, we entertained from eight thirty till nine A.M. and again in the afternoons, when school was out.

I'd taught the rat a trick. He could reach through the bars of his cage and use his own tiny hand to take a scrap of food from the tip of my finger. Only I knew that this had been achieved through accidental starvation of the animal, during those days I had spent sleeping the dope off. Sparky, the dog, was full of his own tricks and the goat, was just different.   The children and their parents visited my gate like it was a small zoo.

The little kids were fine. Beautiful! I enjoyed answering their many questions about the animals in those hazy summer days.

The teenagers were a different matter. There was a chip shop and a "we-sell-everything" newsagent almost straight over the road from me which made eating and shopping very convenient if I didn't want to stray too far from my hole. It was also a good place for a gang of sixteen-year-olds to loiter after dark.

One night, I went over for a chip-butty and I passed the gang at the very moment one youngster was explaining to his mates how running your own hand through the hair at the back of your head felt like an orgasm. I couldn't help but burst out laughing. They all turned to look at me and by way of explanation I shrugged, and said "You've obviously never had an orgasm, mate."

I entered the shop without pausing further, but when I came out with my sandwich they confronted me.

"What did you say to him?"

"Nothing, not important." I found myself facing a gangly youth, inches taller than me, with that unmistakeable, "I want to fight you" look in his eye.

Instantly, the old instincts kicked in and I faced him head on. The rest of the gang snickered, wondering what was going to happen. They saw me as no threat and were prepared to victimise me given half a chance. I did the only thing I knew how and immediately launched the offensive.

"What's your problem mate?"

His small brain ticked over behind glazed eyes. I suspected ecstasy at work, but I should have known better. (E's make you peaceful and loving.) With Tommy it was alcohol which doesn't.

Before anything could develop further, another tall youth with a clean face stepped between us. This was Dan, Dan the Diplomat. He sorted out the explanations and I was able to walk away, but I knew I had made enemies.

Later the same evening, I looked out of my window and saw this same bunch, harassing a small, clean, fat boy. He was walking quickly, obviously trying to get away, whilst they had sent out their smaller front runners to head him off at the pass.

I never could stand around and watch bullying.

I opened the window, and from 150 yards away called out in my most commanding voice, "Oy! Leave him alone!"

All eyes looked up.

I brandished my disconnected phone "Let him go, or I'm calling the police." The boy escaped and I became their focus.

They dispersed fairly soon. The threat of a phone call was too much for their courage, but they didn't leave without curses and insults. A retreating gang must show bravado. It's part of the code.

The rest of the night passed quietly.

Days later, I needed to make a real phone call. I left the

house heading up the hill to the pay-phone. I'd gotten two hundred yards when a voice sang out "Hey mister, your Goat's out".

The goat had made one or two forays from the front gate and was hard to catch once liberated. The road was busy and I feared a traffic accident so I immediately turned on my heels and ran back the way I had come.

There was no escaped goat, just me turning an ankle and sprawling to the ground to shrieks of laughter from the gang. I picked myself up and went to check on the goat. She was safe.

"Right!" I thought, I better see to those little bastards.

Out I went.

They were still hanging around the street, emboldened by their success. I saw them a distance. I walked toward them.

"Hey, mister, your Goat's out again".

Some one should have explained to them that some jokes were only funny once.

I advanced.

They retreated, jeering., "What you following us for you paedophile?"

"I want to know where you live. I'm going to complain to your parents about you."

More jeers as they backed away.

They stopped at a garden.

I assumed it was where one of them lived. I advanced again, they retreated farther; I knocked at the door, a young woman answered.

"No." She had nothing to do with these kids. They were a pest, always sitting on her wall, throwing litter into her garden. I explained the purpose of my visit. Her husband, a strapping fellow, came out. When I explained myself he admitted that he was actually afraid of these boys.

It was time someone confronted them!

He was suffering from depression and it was driving him mad. He believed they came from the local children's home. I thanked him, assured him I would end his problems and carried on with my mission.

At the children's home I was told that these kids (who were by now lurking only yards away) were not from the area. As I was talking to the resident, they came closer and resumed their jeering.

"Hey mister, he's got your goat".

"No lad, I've got your goat!"

..."he hasn't got a goat?" puzzled.

I didn't explain what I meant but left them, promising to call the police.

They followed me home. Inside the house I sat frustrated and phoneless, till there was a knock at the door. It was their spokesman...

Dan the Diplomat.

Recognising him as the boy who had previously acted as peacemaker, I engaged him in conversation. He understood why I had intervened with the bullying, and we spoke like adults for a while. Gradually, one by one the rest of the gang gathered round. Suddenly the garden was thronged with children, sixteen-year-olds, and younger kids who come to see what was happening.

Curtains twitched in the street.

For two hours I talked with them.

My speech was anti-bullying, anti-violence, anti-drugs. They hung onto my every word as I explained the great mysteries. It grew dark as we spoke and their praise for me grew lavish.

They had never been spoken to like this by an adult before and it was late when the eldest finally left with a warm cheerio.

I felt like Jesus Christ.

I was seduced by my power. These chats with the local lads became a daily event. I really couldn't see anything wrong with sitting on my doorstep for two or three hours, holding court with twenty or more youngsters. I came to believe they saw me as some sort of guru with pearls of wisdom dropping from my tongue.

This idea was reinforced, when two of them, a boy and a girl, came to me, and in all seriousness asked me to marry them. Naturally I refused, saying I wasn't a priest or a vicar.

"Well what are you then?"

I honestly answered that I didn't know. Privately, I wondered if I was some sort of messenger or prophet. Which of course, I am.

* * * * * * *

That night in my bedroom, when my hands were green from picking skunk, my mind drifted off. Suddenly, I was chatting to a few of the lads, as if they were in the room with me.

I started arguing with them about drugs.

They wanted some of the skunk.

I wasn't going to give them any. I squashed their arguments with brilliant witticisms. Rhymes and catchphrases were coming out of me at a rapid pace. I realised I was speaking out loud, hearing the boys' half of the conversation only in my head, but replying with my physical voice:

I felt an initial twinge of embarrassment at talking to myself, then I realised, I was alone, and no one could overhear, so I carried on.

I was enjoying it. It felt like human contact and I carried on.

I thought that the phenomenon might be connected to my handling of the skunk; maybe it was being absorbed by my skin, getting me high and imaginative?

Thinking this, I put the skunk aside. I was enjoying the one-on-one chats with my "invisible friends" but I didn't want to go crazy.

Nonetheless, the talking out loud became a habit, and days later, when I had stopped all handling of skunk (which I'd stopped smoking weeks before), I was at it all day and every day, jabbering away as the voice in my head moved faster and faster and I answered it all the more quickly.

I'm in the future going backwards now. That's what it's like when you go mad.

Time twists and turns on you in a hundred dimensions. All of this happened after I left the *blonde* and lots happened before that.

My apologies on with the story! Where was I? Ahh...in hot pursuit of the *blonde*...

* * * * * * *

Chapter 16

I knew she usually went to *Carcroft Club* on Sunday nights. I'd seen her several times there in the early part of the evening but never managed to attract her attention. I later found out that she was part of a crowd that attended *Carcroft* for the band's first set and then habitually left to go to the nearby *Skellow Grange Club* for the second half of the evening.

One night I was out with a couple of the band lads and I steered them to *Carcroft* as a starting place for our drinking session. And there she was.

I moved seats three times so that I could catch her eye: Nothing! It was as if I was invisible. I carried on drinking with my mates, trying to figure out a means of introduction.

When the crowd migrated we followed.

In *The Grange,* I looked around but couldn't see her. I was already set up for sex that night with Catherine Louise McCrum, a girl-next-door type from the next town. I was to visit at her home several miles away after the pubs had shut; when I had finished the "*business*" I had told her I was about.

It wasn't strictly a lie I'd told Catherine. In those clubs, more deals were struck over a pint in the lounge than dry in the committee room.

Moving toward the bar, I saw a surprising sight. Guess who was standing there with his arm around my blonde? Frank Bowkett had pulled her! I sauntered up to offer my congratulations.

"Hey Frank! What you doing with these young birds?"

"Paul! Gimme a break it's me daughter!"

Bliss.

She grinned at me. I smiled back and looked her straight in the face and almost fell over. I had never been close enough to notice her eye colour, and although her hair was like white gold, I knew from her darker brows that it was bottle. I had expected brown eyes, but found myself being scrutinised by twin sparkles of the bluest blue. The *blonde* told me her name and the sound melted on my tongue like chocolate.

I didn't know what to say so accidentally the truth came out. "I can't believe you're Frank's daughter! I've been following you for weeks to try and get a date but you never seemed to notice me. Can I take you out?"

She laughed so hard she spilt her drink. I quickly replaced it with extra for her friends. "Brilliant," she said, after she stopped laughing. "That's the best pick up line I've ever heard. Who are you then?"

I told her my name and that I was the agent for the club she was standing in, that I was manager of the band she was watching.

She spilt her lager again. Then a committee man passed us and complimented me on the band on stage. She stopped laughing and suddenly looked intrigued.

"OK," she said, "you're the band's manager, but that stuff about trying to get a date with me, that was just pure bullshit?"

Over the next fifteen minutes, I described what she had been wearing on the days I had seen her and what band had been performing on those occasions when I had watched her from afar. She was impressed.

Catherine has blue eyes. That night I stared into them and dreamed of the *blonde*.

******

Two days later I took *Claire* out and we spent the night together.

I started seeing her Mondays to Thursdays, still spending weekends at my house with the kids.

She wasn't great in bed but I taught her well. By the time we parted after seven years she had learned everything, and there wasn't much she wouldn't do. I soon discovered that there wasn't much she couldn't do out of bed either.

Before meeting me she had never seen a computer. I showed her mine. Six weeks later she was murdering me at minesweeper. And I can complete the expert level in 120 seconds.

It's a hand-to-eye coordination thing. Mine was good but hers was excellent. Freakish, but not surprising considering who her father was.

I also taught her chess. Within a year she could beat me two times out of five, and every time at blitz. I was playing her at first, enamoured only of her Barbie doll looks. She fell in love with my experience. Then I fell in love with her talent and she played me.

How she beat me at mind games! When she started to gain weight at an alarming rate and I commented, she lost twenty pounds and screwed my seventeen-year-old part-time roadie.

That upset me somewhat and although we reconciled our differences, it marked the beginning of the end.

* * * * * *

Chapter 17

It was two and a half years into the relationship. I had spent those years with the *blonde* as strictly my weekday toy. She knew my son and I knew her two girls, who were both just slightly younger than him. I became midweek-dad to these two, and they became occasional companions of my boy on family outings.

The *blonde* had started out as a strictly egg-and-chips girl but quickly converted to a higher cuisine. We ate out almost every night we met and we ate well. Then when she started to look pregnant and take more interest in minesweeper than in me, I started to feel it was time for a change and that's when I picked on her weight.

At the time, we were sitting in the *Grange* with Wendy.

Wendy! What a woman. She should have been called Peter Pan, because she was the cutest schemingest bitch there ever was. You had to love her.

I knew Wendy from the early days of the first band I managed, *The Gents,* my brother's band. She had been a personal groupie of "Steve Chambers on-Guitar" and had dropped off the scene to have a baby. She claimed Steve was the father but she never told him, although she did tell everybody else.

Wendy resurfaced years later when I was working from *Morton's* club. I met the lady one afternoon, with her two infants in pushchairs. Petite and cute as a kitten under her tilted purple beret, she almost charmed the pants off me right there. I ignored the signals because she was happily married. So she said.

Eight years later when my agency was at its zenith and I was with the *blonde*, she turned up at a gig. She got on well with my new girlfriend and was still happily married. So she said.

The week after, I met her again whilst the *blonde* and I were "on a break". The *blonde* had thrown beer over me for some imagined insult and had stormed out of a club. I'd stormed after her but missed her as she was in the toilet fighting. She usually won her fights, but this time she was up against two, and they took her by surprise. She got her face bashed in and was recovering at home. I was agonising over whether I could end the relationship at such a time. Wendy met me at a gig, consoled me, said how sorry she felt for the *blonde* then took me home and screwed me.

Her happy marriage was a sham. Now she said. Her poor husband was impotent and they slept in separate rooms. Pretty as she was, I found her awkward in bed and I didn't pity him his impotence.

I did pity him his wife though. Wendy started to ring me every day and visit me at my house. I avoided screwing her again for fear of becoming impotent myself. Also I was missing the *blonde* and soon made up with her, telling Wendy the truth, which was that I was uncomfortable cuckolding another man, even an impotent one, and I was missing my old girlfriend.

Wendy seemed to take it well. She wished me health wealth and happiness and like a fool I believed she meant it.

Never trust a gal who smiles sweetly when you leave her. The ones who swear at you are much more honest.

* * * * * * *

The *blonde* took it less well when I told her about Wendy. She was all for putting on the knuckle-dusters, till I persuaded her that a new diamond ring would suit her hand better, and hurt Wendy more. But she swore eternal hatred to the girl, and death to her descendents.

Wendy hovered around the scene for a while and often came close to feeling the toe of the blonde's boot, but after a while she got the message and seemed to fade away.

* * * * * * *

It was over a year before we saw her again. I had enrolled on a college course to take advantage of my grant entitlement before the system changed to student loans. I had completed a year and found it a doddle. I persuaded the *blonde* that she also could do this course and get a hefty grant. She enrolled as a first year student as I was starting year two.

I met her at mid morning break on the first day of term. She was grinning all over her face.

"How did it go?" I asked.

"Great!" she replied, "and I've made a friend. Two friends actually."

"Who are they?"

"You'll know 'em when you see 'em. They'll be here in a minute."   It was Wendy. And also her husband, *Droopy-Kev.*

In my brief fling with Wendy I had mentioned the course I was on, and now here she was, *Droopy* too, cashing in on the grants.

Apparently sufficient time had passed for the *blonde's* death threats to expire and she and Wendy were now hitting it off like long lost sisters. Pretty soon, Wendy was accompanying the *blonde* and me on our nightly outings to see the bands. Kev stayed in to baby-sit Steve Chambers' kid. Wendy took full advantage of *Kev's* softness to flirt with guys at every opportunity.

Then Wendy died her hair blonde and styled it like her friend's. And she started to wear the same kind of clothes. I had no objection to being seen in the company of twin blondes. Especially as I had actually had sex with both of them, and I was happy to let the inevitable rumour that we were a full blown three-some develop amongst my colleagues.

I loved watching them dance together. They used to tease outrageously, touching each others bodies and even kissing each other in a raunchy floor show for the watching guys, but they always went home with me.

Everybody thought I was a lucky bastard. This of course is what I am. Why else would I be chosen?

* * * * * *

We usually went together back to the *blonde's* house where we would sit and laugh until the taxi came. Sometimes I would take Wendy home in the car. It was a half hour trip and it gave us the chance to talk. Every time I had a tiff with the *blonde*, I would unload on Wendy's sympathetic ear.

Sometimes the *blonde* and I had big blow outs and I wouldn't speak to her for days. At these times, I would spend hours on the phone to Wendy, until the *blonde* and I were reconciled and the three musketeers were back on the road.

All the time, Wendy was growing more and more like the *blonde*. I didn't worry about it, it was fun. But alarm bells started ringing when one day the *blonde* returned from visiting Wendy's house and told me she had decorated her living room the same as ours. Still we laughed it off. What harm could it do?

I grew very close to Wendy. I suppose I had developed a crush. But I remembered our one dry act of fucking and it never went any further. I started to really like her though, and when she asked me if I knew of any work her school-leaving step-son Rick could do for the holidays before he went to University, I bent over backwards to create a job. We could afford an extra roadie.

Rick was a good-looking smart young kid. He had a girlfriend who nobody, including himself, liked much, and at seventeen, he was still a virgin.

I called the *blonde* fat once too often and she decided to teach me a lesson. Soon Rick wasn't a virgin anymore, although I didn't discover this until several weeks after his initiation.

During those weeks, the *blonde* had been looking much better and I had started to fancy her again. But despite her new trim figure, sexual relations between us began to cool.

I'd learned by now that it's a mistake to press for sex in these situations, so when she'd go off to bed early after a night in watching TV, the most I would do would be to go up soon after her and snuggle up, hoping that something might develop. It didn't.

It wasn't that I was feeling desperately horny. Horniness in me usually starts only after physical contact. I felt desire though; a desire to become horny. And I did feel concerned about the lack of sex. I always believed that sex must be a regular part of any healthy relationship. Fair enough there will always be times when you're both too tired or drunk or full of food. But if a couple who are attracted to each other sleep in the same bed for four nights running, and they don't get down to sex at some point, it seems to me there's something wrong.

The pattern became that I would meet the *blonde* on Sunday nights at the club where we would drink together and return to her house. Being drunk, we would both fall asleep cuddling, no sex. In the early morning I would awaken and lie there bored for two hours hoping she would wake up and that intimacy would begin.

No matter how long I waited, she would sleep on until I got up and went downstairs to potter about for a while before I went to work. If I was still around when she got up, I was too careful to suggest we go back to bed. I'd already got the message that she didn't feel like it today so I would just stick around as long as I could, hoping she might change her mind.

Mondays Tuesdays Wednesdays and Thursdays would pass

like this. By the time Friday came, I would be thinking "Tonight's the night... we've not done it for a week, she's bound to be feeling the urge by now" and I would hang around longer, certain that she would initiate. After all, we wouldn't be seeing each other now for two more days. And there was no guarantee that the ongoing situation would change by Monday morning.

When hours had passed and it still hadn't happened, I'd make my own move and be amazed to find her pushing me away.

One time, I asked her, playfully, if she was saving herself for someone else and met a furiously indignant response; *what sort of a slag did I take her for?* Just because she didn't feel sexual at the moment did not mean she was the type who slept around. Fuck off!

I would leave feeling baffled and would spend my working hours composing long letters to her, explaining my insecurities, telling her that it wasn't that I just wanted her for sex, but that I was concerned our relationship was dying without it. These letters were never sent, but I would use the content later on when we discussed the subject.

All she did was assure me that things were absolutely fine between us. She just didn't feel sexual at the moment...not just with me but with anybody...maybe we should take a break? She needed some space.

I gave her space.

I started sleeping at home some weekday nights, which gave me extra time to do my work. I would always phone her before bedtime though, and we would usually have a long chat.

One night I phoned and got no answer. Not on her land line, not on her mobile. A feeling that something was wrong crept in.

I drove the seven miles to where she lived. The lights were on. It was around midnight. I knocked at the door.

The *blonde* answered from behind it, "What do you want?"

What do you want? I was stunned.

She'd been my girlfriend for almost three years and I used to stay there four nights a week. And she asks me what I want!

"I want to come in."

"Hang on a minute." She fussed around behind the frosted

glass. Then I saw a figure behind her. A man's figure.

"Open that fucking door right now or I'll break it down."
It opened. There stood Rick.
"Babe, it's not what you think..."
I didn't stop to think. I just grabbed Rick in a headlock, ready to batter the shite out of him. There was no cool blooded calculation in that assault. No martial finesse. I just grabbed him.
"Stop it, stop it! What are you doing? He only gave me a lift home and came in for a coffee..."
Suddenly I felt stupid. There I was, a mature man of substance, turning up unannounced in the dead of night, out of control with jealousy, and assaulting a seventeen year old boy, when the very idea that my twenty six year old beauty would consider screwing this school-kid was ridiculous. I let go of him.
I was still angry. I shouted at him to get out and not bother turning up to collect his wages. He left sheepishly and the *blonde* and I were alone.
She was grinning everywhere.
"What's so funny?" I demanded to know.
"You," she said, "look at you. You're all jealous over Rick. I can't believe you!" Shaking her head and smiling. "Come on lets go to bed."
After our lovemaking, which was better than it had been for ages, she persuaded me what a fool I was and that I should apologise to Rick and let him keep his job. Which is exactly what I did.
For the next two weeks my sex life improved.
When I apologised to Rick, I also told him he'd been foolish to find himself at that hour in the house of a more or less married woman. Any man would assume they were screwing each other. Then he expressed great grief at the idea that I could think he would do such a thing to me after all I had done for him. We hugged like brothers and I gave him a pay rise.
Did I mention that Rick was Wendy's step-son? Yes I think I did. Did I also mention that she was a scheming bitch? Yes, she was. Rick, in fact, was *Kev's* son from a previous marriage, in which he was presumably less droopy than he is now.
Two weeks later, the *blonde* and I were preparing to go out

for Saturday lunch. I'd been hinting that we should have sex first as I knew that after a feed, the snake would want only to sleep. She had chosen instead to sit playing computer games until it was time for our food.

I saw a couple of unopened letters on the desk, and to kill a little time as I waited for her to improve her personal best, I opened one. It was the mobile phone bill and it was massive. I started to check the call list.

I had given the *blonde* her own mobile phone on my business account. A tax dodge. The big bill was for use of that phone.

One number stood out. Long calls, regular calls. The same number, again and again and again. I muttered about this under my breath. There was something familiar about this number.

I sometimes used the *blonde's* phone to make business calls while we were out and assumed that this was the nature of these multiple calls. But I couldn't work out who I had been ringing so often, "Hmmm...who's number is that...I've made forty seven calls to it in a month and I don't know who.....?"

I was interrupted by the blonde sweeping me off my feet and onto the bed.

"What the fuck ...?"

"Well babe, if you want some sex before we go out we better get started hadn't we...?"

It wasn't my birthday but I took the gift. "Woohoo!" All my patience had paid off and the *blonde's* sexuality had returned with dividends. We had a quick but satisfying shag and left for lunch.

I forgot all about the mobile phone bill and went to bed early at my own house, having dropped the *blonde* off at hers. I slept well, until three AM when suddenly I sat bolt upright eyes wide open. I knew who's that number was.

It was Rick's!

I got out the bill which was several pages long, and highlighted every entry of his number. I could account for me calling him once or twice from that phone, but not forty seven times. And sometimes the calls were over an hour long. I checked the dates with my diary. Always, they coincided with times I was not with the *blonde*.

I drove to her house. It was six AM. It was dewy, crisp and misty. The birds were welcoming the sun, as I stood at her door step wondering what to say.

I called her number.

"What's up babe?" answered a voice husky with sleep and tinged with concern.

"I think you know. We need to talk." She came straight to the door in her nightdress and all I wanted to do was kiss her.

Inside, upstairs, I asked her straight out what was going on. She played dumb. Said she hadn't a clue about those calls. I got out the bill.

I showed her with yellow highlighter where the calls were. Dates. Duration of call. Cost. Then I showed I showed her my diary.

I always kept a diary showing what gig I had attended each night, and we both knew which nights I had seen her, and when she'd been alone with the phone. Eventually she admitted making the calls.

"He's just a good friend babe. I just like to talk to him."

"For three hours at midnight last Tuesday after I left here?"

"Yes."

"What about?"

"Oh, you know...problems...his girlfriend problems...my worries with you...we just talk...we're just good friends."

"What about the time he was in you're house?"

"He just gave me a lift home... He often does that when I'm out with Wendy."

"How often?"

"I don't know!" She was getting angry now. "Look, don't be so fucking stupid! If you think I'm that kind of slag that would fuck a seventeen-year old, you can fuck off, get out of my house, now! Go on. Fuck off!" Trembling I stood my ground.

"OK, but my next call will be to Rick, and he won't like what I've got to say."

"Listen babe..." Calmer now. Momentary elation. I'd got her!

"There's no need for that... I love you... You've got nothing to worry about. Just let me get some sleep OK? Don't be going round to Rick's causing trouble when he's done nothing. You'll just make yourself look a fool."

"Has he ever stayed in this house?"

A pause, while she considered what I might already know, or was sure to discover.

"He slept here once. We got dropped off in a taxi and he came in for coffee. He meant to get another taxi back but there weren't any."

"Where did he sleep?"

A grin.

"On this bed."

"With you?"

"I said on this bed, not in it. He slept here and I slept there. We just went to sleep, no touching, no kissing, no holding hands. That's all. In the morning, he was really embarrassed, in case you came round and he went off dead early without even waking me up... You know what I'm like in the mornings."

We haggled back and forth for a while until 10 AM. Now the children were getting up. Eventually I could see she was falling asleep on me as we spoke. I left, arranging to pick her up for lunch a few hours later.

As soon as I was in the car, I phoned Rick. With choice words I rousted him from his bed and he met me outside my house.

He approached me with open arms. "Mate, mate how can you think this of me?"

"My office. Now!"

I closed the door behind us and sat opposite him, reverse mounted on a hard back chair, while he sat nervously eyeing the door.

"Rick, I'm sitting like this at a distance from you so you'll feel safe. If I try to grab you, I've first got to get out from behind this chair, and by the time I do that you can be out the door... tell me the truth now, man to man... What's been going on? Tell me the truth like a man. I promise, I won't touch you."

"Nothing, nothing! We just chat on the phone and I give her a few lifts...how can you think...?"

"Cut the crap Rick. She's already admitted to me she slept with you at least once. I think it's more than that."

Huge pause. I could see the cogs ticking.

"I don't believe you." Wrong answer.

I edged forward and held his eye with steel.

"I'm going to make a phone call. One sound from you and you won't make it through that door. Get it?"

My position on the chair was a false security blanket for him. In *Goshin-Jitsu*, we studied what we called "weapons of convenience." Pool cues, glasses, ash-trays, and chairs. The sort of tools you might find handy in a bar room brawl. I was holding the chair with my arms crossed over, resting at wide angles apart, one hand high on the back, the other low at the joint of the back and the base. This allows you to stand quickly and flip the chair from under you turning it into a powerful club. During *Idle* times at gigs I'd explained this manoeuvre to Rick, as he'd shown a great interest in the sport, and now he recognised it.

His face turned a paler shade of white. "OK."

"Don't move!"

I punched up the *blonde's* speed dial number on the hands-free set mounted two feet away on the wall. Three rings and she answered. Sleepy voice. Annoyed.

"What's up now?"

"Hi babe, it's me. Sorry to wake you up but I just cant get my head round this. You say you slept with Rick, in your bed, just the once?"

"Yes." Curt. Without hesitation.

"OK, Love, I just wanted to get that straight. You can go back to sleep now. See you later." I cut the line.

"Well?" A long pause.

"I don't believe that was Claire. You could have just called anybody."

I sighed and shook my head. Another wrong answer.

To confuse a witness, feign boredom. It always works.

"Quiet!"

I punched the number up again. She answered, "Hello?"

"Sorry...who's that?" Me, feigning surprise.

"It's me. Who do you think it is?"

"Is that really you, babe?"

"Yes dickhead! What do you want now?"

"Sorry babe, I meant to ring one of the lads up about tonight's gig. I must have hit re-dial by mistake. So sorry I woke you again. I'll let you get back to sleep."

"Well, I'm up now, you might as well talk to me. Where we going for dinner?"

We chatted on for a while whilst Rick grew smaller and smaller in the corner. Eventually I made excuses of being busy-busy and we hung up.

"OK, Rick, now do you believe me?" He believed me.

"Right Rick. You know she's admitted to sleeping with you once, but I don't believe that's all it was. Tell me the truth now, and you can keep your job until you leave for college. But the first thing that comes out of your mouth that sounds like a lie and you're through! You can forget last weeks wages as well as next, and I might just lose my temper."

He shook his head looking at the floor. "I can't believe she's told you," was all he could manage, but gradually I got out of him everything that I already knew must be true. They had been sleeping together for weeks. She had taken his virginity and they had had sex more than once. Strangely, he couldn't remember how many times.

I asked him what his future intentions were.

"What do you mean?"

"Do you love her? Do you want her to be your girlfriend? Do you intend to carry on seeing her?"

He answered a vehement NO! to all these questions. That pissed me off for several reasons, so I pissed him off.

"The truth is, Rick, that she didn't ever admit to having sex with you. She just said she'd slept in the same bed, but nothing happened."

"Doh!"

I swear he said Doh! Just like Homer Simpson.

"You're going away to college soon, Rick. I don't ever expect to see you again after that. For now, you can do your remaining gig, (that night's was to be his last), and you can say a goodbye to the lads. You had a fling with my woman, now it's over and you're going away. I don't want you to tell her you admitted it all to me. She's my girlfriend and I want to stay with her. I might even marry her. So from now on you have nothing to do with her. OK?"

"OK." He had been nodding vigorously as I spoke.

"Oh, Rick, one more thing."

"What's that?" Still nodding.

I wanted to hit him, but I'd made a promise and I always keep my promises, (another reason I was chosen). I just spoke, coldly and calmly, but with iron in my voice.

"You're an asshole, Rick. I don't blame you for taking your chance with her; she's a beautiful, sexy woman. Who wouldn't have done what you did? You're not an asshole for that. But after I found you together, you should have come clean. Not humiliated me like you did, making me apologise and then giving me all the crap about 'how can you think this of me, mate?'... and now, today, you've sat there and told me lie after bare-faced lie."

Rick said nothing. His nodding had stopped too.

"If at any point, Rick, you could have admitted the truth without making me prove it first, I could have some respect for you, but now I've got none. None! You're an asshole Rick, a total asshole."

I was going to punch him in the face, despite my promise, but by now he'd shrunk to a size too small to hit, and believe it or not in that moment I almost pitied him. Only almost though. I continued:

"I forgive you for screwing my bird, Rick, although I should kick your face in. But I'm a man of my word and you can go.... but if I ever see you again, you better get out of the way quick. If I walk into a room and you're in it, then you get up and leave OK?"

He couldn't speak. He just nodded up and down again.

"That's all. Get out." I opened the door and made a sideways gesture with my thumb. The relief on his face was palpable.

I stole the line about "leaving rooms" from a Jack Higgins novel, and I'd waited years to use it on someone. I felt elated. Rick left without another word.

My next call was to Wendy.

* * * * * * *

Wendy had been my friend, my closest confidante, to whom I'd expressed all my fears about the *blonde* having it off with another man. I knew that she and the *blonde* were as thick as thieves. It was impossible she couldn't have known.

I summoned her to my quarters and gave her the low down.

"No!" she said. No way was Rick seeing the *blonde*.

"He's admitted it, Wendy."

"No way. I don't believe you. She would never... Rick would never..."

I showed her the phone bill and her face turned grey, which made me believe she too had been duped. The next hour was filled with Wendy expressing her anger at the *blonde* for seducing her step-son. She would not have him! He was going to college and would never see the *blonde* again. Wendy would see to that. I could count on her. We left it at that.

I met the *blonde* for lunch. She was far away in her thoughts. Nervous and upset. At this time I believed that she was unaware of Rick's full confession. I had sworn both him and Wendy to silence, and I trusted the authority I felt I wielded.

It was a strange situation. I knew the truth, the *blonde* knew the truth, but I didn't think she knew that I knew that. But she did. This fact, and more, came out a year later, when I finally managed to manipulate her into a situation in which she had to be honest with me.

On this day though, we were both quiet and thoughtful. We attended that night's gig together. Wendy too. Rick was also there doing his roadie thing. I started to get drunk on whiskey.

Sitting there, next to the *blonde,* facing Rick across the table, my thoughts became a carousel. All of us sitting there, everybody pretending everything was normal.

Towards the end of the evening, it got too much for me, and whilst the *blonde* was in the toilets, I told Rick he had better disappear. He didn't need telling twice.

I told the lads I'd let him go home early as it was his last night, and he had to get up early for college the next day. I told the *blonde* the truth later in bed and we cried together over what had been done.

Then we reconciled. A new closeness grew between us and I decided to move in with her so that I could see her every day. We did up the spare room for my son, who said "goodbye" to those intimate weekends alone with dad, in favour of weekends in *Carcroft* with a new room and ready-made playmates.

The truth was, that after the Rick affair, I couldn't bear to let her out of my sight. The relationship changed. Previously, she had been the one chasing me, now, I was the one chasing her. But we were OK for a while.

I started to accompany her on all her outings, sitting out dull hours in nightclubs awaiting the two AM lights- up. I had never been interested in visiting nightclubs unless it was for business or pulling birds. I don't dance, didn't drink well, and in those days, I didn't smoke. The music is so loud in those places, it denies any conversation, so my entertainment options were rather narrowed down. I found myself very bored, watching the clock, as the girlies gyrated on the dance-floor, or spent ages in the lavatories where they took e's or snorted coke. Another thing I couldn't share in.

Gradually I started to come to terms with the idea of letting her back off the leash, and one Wednesday, when the three musketeers were scheduled for a night out at *Berlins*, I decided to give it a rain check, and allow the *blonde* and Wendy out alone. Provided she returned by normal time, i.e., by half past two.

It worked! Here she was, fresh and frisky, and on time. I was waiting. We had a fine romp and slept like babies. The same thing happened the following week, and the week after.

The fourth week, she wasn't home till half past three, and when she arrived, she went straight to the toilet for ten minutes, before going straight up to bed.

She said she had been waiting for a taxi that didn't arrive, and then she had felt sick, so the cab had to stop, making her even later. I knew this couldn't be true and asked her to level with me.

I was straight John Bull when I said to her that whatever she told me I would forgive anything, as long as I got the truth. I could handle the idea of a momentary lapse into infidelity, but not the thought of being lied to and made a fool of.

All she did was get mad and accuse me of paranoia. I went downstairs.

Being paranoid, I called the taxi firm she had used. I told them I was worried about my girlfriend who was out late and had called me earlier to say she was waiting for a cab which was already on its way. That had been almost an hour ago and she wasn't home yet. The man checked the log and told me where and when she had been collected. Then he told me that she was OK because she had a guy with her at the time. I thanked him for his understanding and hung up.

I said nothing to the *blonde* about this. I knew it would lead to denial and more arguments. I spent a sleepless night thinking what to do. I decided I'd had enough.

It was clear to me that despite our new closeness, she was back up to her old tricks, and I wasn't prepared to take it lying down. I could just have left, but that would leave a huge gap in my life, and I wanted closure. I decided on revenge.

At about this time, the blonde was planning a "Blackpool-trip." A Blackpool-trip involved a dozen or more of the local girls going off for the weekend to the infamous West-Coast seaside resort. They would arrive by mid Saturday afternoon, book into bed and breakfast, don their glad-rags and hit the town.

Blackpool is a sex town. People visit the Golden Mile, which is a mile-long strip of bars discos and pubs along the sea front. These places are crowded all year round with revellers of all ages, hellbent on having a good time with members of the opposite sex. The girls did this trip two or three times a year, telling their boyfriends they were "only out for a laugh" and that nothing would happen.

In reality, they indiscriminately got up to every sexual antic imaginable. As with the band nights, the chances of gossip reaching home were negligible, and the girls had a saying among themselves: "what goes on the mile, stays on the mile."

Of course, I knew exactly what was what, having entertained many times in Blackpool during my days on the road. The other local lads had a pretty good idea about it too. They sometimes arranged their own trips. But for the sake of survival of the species they turned a blind eye. Also, the girls tended to return home in extra horny mood, having experienced new delights to fuel their fantasies, so it wasn't a total loss.

I waited till the *blonde* had departed for the coast, wishing her a good time with a fond kiss farewell, then I put on my pulling shirt and went out. I had a few steady pints at the club, carefully watching the crowd for a suitable subject.

The club I was in was *Skellow Grange*, very local to the *blonde's* house. We were both well known there. No chance of getting off with anyone who knew her. It wasn't that the village girls wouldn't do such a thing out of moral objection. It happened all the time with other people, being kept hush-hush for a while and only sparking a minor row when the truth did inevitably emerge in the fullness of time. If I'd been living with any other girl from the village I could have had my pick of beauties whilst she was away. The *blonde* however was one violent psycho-bitch from hell, and well known for it.

Twice I had to appear in court as a witness to her innocence, after she'd battered some young thing for one reason or other. Upset Bowkett, she put the boot in first and asked questions later. In her village, not even the dogs would have touched me with a bargepole. I needed a stranger.

I spotted her at the bar. She was pretty enough but not outstanding, and well on the plump side of pudgy. Perfect. A fatty wouldn't be too choosy.

I ordered at the bar before her, having pushed the queue, then, noticing her annoyance after it was too late, and my beer was already being pulled, I said to the barmaid, "...and get this young lady whatever she wants."

I dazzled her with charm and flattery for ten minutes before the bar closed and we were about to be asked to leave. Then I played my trump card. "Do you fancy a pizza?" Always play to their weakness. Before we reached the pizza store, I betrayed my true intentions.

"Listen," I said, "I don't really want a pizza, I want to screw the arse off you, how about it?"

Once you've established you're an OK guy fellows, it's OK to come out with a line like that. Don't worry. She knows your agenda from the opening gambit, and has similar ideas herself. Stating your intentions at this stage won't alarm her, it will just confirm what she already hopes for, and boost her ego. She may not go along with the suggestion that first night, but she won't be offended, and she might just agree. This one did.

I went one further and told her that my girlfriend had been a right bitch to me, by sleeping around behind my back. That she was away tonight and I wanted revenge by screwing someone else in her bed. It was tonight or not at all. Was she interested? You bet!

I gave her a quick feel on the walk back over the field. Just so she wouldn't go off the boil in the few minutes the walk would take. She was all over me there and then, dragging me to the floor. I went along with it for a while, then asked her what we were doing on the wet grass while there was a warm bed waiting. Off we went.

I sneaked her in past the babysitter.

Here's irony: The kid sitting was Wendy's son. The one she blamed on "Steve-Chambers-on-guitar." He was sleeping, or looked asleep.

In the bedroom we went through the Kama-Sutra. She made an awful lot of noise. I had my usual first-night-not-stand erection problem, but I made up for it with other skills. After an hour or so I sneaked her out and walked her home. Or rather to the friends house she was staying at. She wasn't a village local or it never would have happened.

Satisfied, I awaited the *blonde's* return the following day, and gleefully screwed away at her after hearing how dull Blackpool had been. I hadn't changed the bed and I was hoping she would pick up on some trace of strange perfume or a lipstick mark on the sheets, but she was oblivious.

For three weeks she behaved frustratingly well, acquiescing to my every whim, thanking me for being so trusting as to allow her to come and go as she pleased, without giving her the third degree.

I was encouraged by this and thought we might actually have a future. Now I regretted what I had done. But I thought I'd gotten away with it.

She hadn't gotten away with her adventure of six weeks earlier though, and it gnawed at my mind. It had to be out in the open and explained if she and I were to continue as a couple. After a while I broached the subject.

We were sitting cosily on the settee, and to all appearances, all was well with our world. I felt there could be trust between us, and choosing this intimate moment, I played my opening.

"Babe...?"

"Yes babe?"

"You know when you were late home from the nightclub a

few weeks ago and you told me you'd been sick in the taxi?"

"Oh yeah?" suspicious now.

"That night, I called the taxi firm, they told me that when they picked you up you were with a guy."

The rest of the conversation is not fit for print. She grew furious and accused me of spying on her. There was no guy! No guy at all! She was on her own, and she was sick!

Wrong answer.

If she had given me the truth at this point, I'd have stayed. But I knew she was lying and I left, deciding to end the relationship permanently and take my satisfying secret with me.

I spent a lonely three weeks working hard with no word from the *blonde*. I took a couple of different girls home some nights and we fooled around, but I was missing her. Then one evening the phone rang.

"Who's this fucking bitch you've had in my bed? When I find out there's gonna be a blood bath round here!"

I just smiled and said hello.

It seemed that the fourteen-year-old baby-sitting-boy had been awake after all, and he had heard everything.

Sweet Irony. After a period of self preservation motivated silence, then thinking me off the scene for good, he had conscientiously downloaded to his mother, the lovely and considerate Wendy, the story of his dreadful experience.

Wendy of course, was the step-mother of my young cuckold and I thought; life is sweet, it doesn't get better than this!

The *blonde* was persistent. My phone wouldn't stop ringing no matter how many times I laughed and hung up. Eventually I made a deal. I would tell her my secrets if she would tell me hers. Truth for truth. She must go first, and I promised her that the first thing that came out of her mouth that sounded like a lie, the phone would go down! A useful phrase in an argument with a liar.

In the course of two hours conversation, the phone went down several times. Every time she veered from what I thought probable, I hung up. Each time she called me back immediately, and we continued. Gradually I uncovered an incredible, but believable account of her misdeeds.

Yes, she had seen Rick on the night she was late. Yes it was him in the taxi. No, they didn't have sex...she hadn't even touched him.... The phone went down... Five minutes later: OK, they'd kissed and stuff but nothing else. What kind of a girl did I think she was? The phone almost went down again but I was laughing too much and couldn't press the button. Eventually I got the full story and now it was my turn.

"So what was the name of this bitch you did in my bed? My fucking bed!"

I truthfully answered that I didn't know. I had to put the phone on the other side of the room while she ranted away finding combinations of swear words I didn't know were possible. Then I asked a question.

"Now that you've done with all that, how do you fancy a shag?"

An hour later I was in her bed, as she performed spectacularly to ensure she outdid the previous occupant. The young tell-tale had done me proud in his description of his aural ordeal, and the *blonde* had the impression I had performed like a stud.

If only she knew.

After this, she and I settled back down together. Everything was out in the open you see, and now that I knew that she had been persuaded into lesbian sex by Wendy and given Wendy's toy-boy (a school friend of Rick's) a double headed blow-job in the nightclub car park, while I had been waiting at home, I was quite happy with my position.

Most people couldn't have dealt with this, but I can deal with and forgive anything as long as I am told the truth. I can accept infidelity as an inevitable consequence of dating mischievous women, but I will not tolerate being lied to. More reasons for being chosen.

It also came out that Wendy had known about the *blonde's* affair with Rick all the time. More than that, she had been instrumental in starting the episode, encouraging the *blonde* in that direction, and even minding her children whilst they met. Wendy had also been constantly encouraging the *blonde* to leave me, at the very time I had been pouring my heart out to Wendy over the phone, and assuring me that my girlfriend only had eyes for me.

When I told my lover about the long chats I had enjoyed with Wendy, we both saw instantly that the little bitch had done her best to split us up. We concluded that the motives behind this were jealousy and revenge.

Suddenly, the *blonde* wanted to go straight round and murder her best mate. She didn't do that, but she ended the friendship, and for weeks it was just me and my blonde together.

I felt bitter about the Rick affair for a long time. Always it preyed on my mind. I had to keep asking the blonde about little details: What they had done? How they had done it? Where? And where was I at the time?

Sometimes this angered her and she would refuse to discuss the subject. At other times though, she seemed to enjoy telling me things. Particularly whilst we were making love. Gradually, she revealed more and more small infuriating details, and as the full extent of the picture grew clearer by the week, a deep anger that I hadn't previously encountered in myself began to form. But I put it aside.

With Wendy off the scene, the *blonde* and I had found a new togetherness. With all our secrets in the open we felt clean. We were purified and in love. I proposed marriage, she accepted and we had started to try for a baby.

When she didn't catch on straight away we went for tests. Both of us checked out OK, but still she didn't conceive.

It seems that some things are simply not meant to be.

* * * * * * *

It was just as well in the end, as after a year of our new closeness, the bubble burst. We had set a date for the following May, a year in advance. This gave us plenty of time to plan a big wedding and to save up the cash to pay for it. We bought the rings. Two plain gold bands. We felt happy.

Jokingly, she suggested that for her hen-night, she would like to go with all her female friends for a weeks holiday in Magaluf. Jokingly, I said fine. A few days later, in the course of my work I was chatting to a barmaid at one of my venues and was told how much she was looking forward to the Magaluf trip.

I thought it was an extension of the joke, and played along

saying how it would be fine, as obviously all the girls would behave themselves like virgin saints. The barmaid laughed her tits off and I went home chuckling too.

When I told the *blonde* the joke she said, "What's funny? We're going!"

"No way!"

For my transatlantic readers, I must explain that Magaluf is a holiday resort on the island of Majorca, famous for its wild nightlife. Only young single people go there, and they go there for one reason. To get laid. Magaluf dwarfs even Blackpool in its reputation for licentious lewd behaviour. So much so that it is nick-named "Shagaluf".

A hen night is the British equivalent of a bachelor party for girls. Traditionally the girls go off on a one night pub crawl, ending up at a night-club, and all getting very drunk. Sometimes they will book a male strip-o-gram for the bride to be, and take embarrassing photos of her doing things like licking whipped cream of the stud's chest, or having her backside covered in baby oil. Some girls go even further and actually do get laid. Theoretically it's their last night of freedom before accepting the ball and chain of wedded bliss.

Knowing the blonde's promiscuous history, I had little doubt she might discreetly do the latter on a standard localised hen party, but at least there was a doubt. She might and she might not.

Sending her to the sun drenched hot spot of Shagaluf left no question that she would not only get laid, but would be involved in wild group sex and orgies. I would be standing at the alter on my wedding day knowing this had happened. Also every single guest would know, and would be laughing behind their hands as we took our vows. I wasn't having it and said so.

"You're not going to Magaluf."

"I am and that's that."

"Then there'll be no wedding."

"Fine."

"Fine!"

"Fine!!"

And that was that, the wedding was off.

So was the Magaluf trip because without me to finance it, it couldn't happen. From that moment, the relationship deteriorated.

I was a control freak who thought she was a slag. I didn't trust her, so I couldn't love her.

How could I trust her given the track record she had? I tried to explain that I generally did trust her to be good, or at least discreet, in normal situations, but a week in Magaluf with the girls was not a normal situation and I didn't trust it.

"So...you're saying that I can never go on holiday with my friends...is that it?"

"No, I'm not saying that. I just don't want to feel lousy on our wedding day thinking what you might have just been up to without me."

"What are you trying to say? That I'll just go there and shag every bloke in sight?"

I was trying to say exactly that but it wasn't a good idea to do so. I just shrugged and stayed silent. She stormed out.

Soon, she was going out with the girls again and returning very late. At first, I had accompanied her on her nightclub outings, but I couldn't keep the pace up.

Claire was an occasional recreational drug user. I had known this about her from the start, and although I mildly disapproved, I tolerated it.

For nightclub trips, she and her friends would share a bag of speed, or when they could get it, cocaine. They also took ecstasy. This meant that they could go out as early as seven in the evening and still be feeling brand new in the small hours of the next morning.

I kept finding myself out in the company of four or five girls, all high on coke, still hitting the dance floors at 2:30 when DJ stopped. Then they would want to party on at one or the other's house. I was welcome to tag along and they all gave me plenty of attention as I was usually paying for the drinks, but by midnight I was usually pooped.

As I've said, I don't dance, if I drank more than a few beers, I just fell to sleep, and the loud music of the clubs destroys any chance of conversation. I found myself very bored.

After a short while, I started to stay in and amused myself playing internet chess until the *blonde's* return from her late-nighters. Playing in the MSN game rooms became very entertaining, and sometimes I would still be there long after the *blonde* had returned home and gone to bed. I suppose I became addicted. I built up my screen personality into a chatty jokey chess expert, who often had the whole room in fits of laughter. I didn't really notice the *blonde* getting later and later on her expeditions until one day when they went out for Tracey's birthday.

Tracey had taken over as the *blonde's* shadow soon after Wendy vanished from the scene. As with Wendy I had enjoyed the onlooker's suppositions that I was getting simultaneous attention from them both. Also, as with Wendy, Tracy became my confidant, to whom I unloaded occasional grievances over the *blonde,* and I started to think of her as being in some way mine, although nothing else developed.

On Tracey's birthday, my two beauties were showing off their fancy dress costumes. Short grey skirts that showed their stocking tops. White blouses showing a lot of cleavage, and hair tied into pigtails with red ribbon. A pair of naughty schoolgirls. They looked fantastic. I made up my mind to drop the chess the minute she walked back in and grab a piece of the action.

The sun was up before I saw her again, and when she arrived she went straight to bed. I followed her up and climbed in next to her. I put my hand between her legs and knew immediately she'd been up to no good. She was sopping wet.

I said nothing, just took my dues.

In the morning, I gently quizzed her about her night. She told me they had all gone on to an "open-all-night" club, after the normal club closed, it had been a dull night there so she had returned home leaving the other girls partying.

The following day she was out somewhere and Tracey called in to say hello. I told her my worries about the *blonde* and asked her if she would be honest enough to tell me the truth about their outing. I promised confidentiality. She agreed and told me that after the nightclub, the *blonde* was tired so they dropped her off at another friends house, where she slept (alone) till six AM, when she awoke and returned to me.

I knew this couldn't be true. There was no logic in it. Why would the blonde sleep alone a mile away from home when she could easily have returned to her own bed?

Also there was no logic in her being sleepy at that time when I knew they had been on cocaine. You don't sleep on coke.

And whether it was true or not, it totally contradicted the *blonde's* story of having gone to the all-nighter with them.

I thanked Tracey and kept my thoughts to myself.

Whatever the truth was it wasn't in either of the stories I had been told. I didn't discuss it further with the *blonde* immediately. If I breached Tracey's confidence my information source would dry up and at the same time, I would betray to the *blonde* the fact that Tracey and I shared secrets. Fatal!

Instead, I waited until we were making love and the *blonde* was in a particularly horny mood, before asking if she would put on her fancy dress outfit for me. I saw a mischievous look come into her eyes as she agreed.

Hungrily I watched as she donned the stockings, the skirt, blouse and ribbons, and then applied glossy red lipstick. Dressed like this she straddled my face and when I paused for air after some minutes under the grey pleats, I tried my luck.

"You've done this before in this skirt haven't you babe?"

"What do you mean?" she said, grinning.

"Listen babe, I don't mind. In fact it makes me horny. But I know that when you went out for Tracey's birthday in these clothes you came back dripping wet. I know you were up to more than you told me, all I want is to hear about it."

"Don't be stupid!" but she was too horny to move away. I licked some more bringing her close to the point. Then I tried again.

"You want to know how I know?"

"There's nothing to know. Don't stop!"

"I know, because Tracey called around the next day, while you were out, and without realising it she dropped you in it. She told me that you had not gone to the all-nighter but had slept at Sarah's house."

"She's lying!" thrusting at my mouth.

I just laughed.

"If she's lying, let's call her up right now. I'll make the call as if you're not here, and I'll ask her to tell me again what happened. She was obviously trying to protect you from being found out but she made a clumsy job of it. It wasn't her fault. I took her by surprise. You know how clever I am."

I was horny as hell myself, and moved her down to where

we touched in the middle, so she could see how hard I was.

"See babe...I really don't mind...If I was mad about it I would have said something before, but I wanted to enjoy hearing from you what you did. Come on, tell me the truth, I wont be mad."

She knew she was cornered and grinned. She was one very horny woman. I almost said lady.

"OK, I'll tell you the truth but you promise you won't get mad 'cos its all in the past now isn't it?"

"OK," slipping into her.

As she rode me she told how she, Tracey, and her own cousin, Sarah, had picked up a bunch of guys who were staying at the *Formula-One*. A cheap motel used mainly by prostitutes.

They had gone back to the guy's rooms. Sarah was with one guy, Tracey with another. Those two girls were both single so there was nothing wrong with that was there?

Sarah had gone off to one room where she shagged her guy. Tracey and the *blonde* had gone into another room where the *blonde* had rolled a joint, while Tracey shagged her man. The other guys had all gone off to their own rooms and the *blonde* had wandered about the corridors waiting for the others to finish up. She then went back into Tracey's guy's room where he was wanting "another go". Tracey gave him a second condom and he was fumbling to put it on, so my *blonde* put the condom on for him. That's all that happened. Honest.

All? I was furious. Firstly, even if that was all that had happened, it was enough to incense me. Secondly, the story itself was incredible:

A bunch of guys pull three kinkily dressed girls. Two of the guys go to their rooms screwing, while the others go off to bed, leaving the spare girl to amuse herself?

No way could that be true.

And then the *blonde* had simply put a condom onto a guy's penis, without giving him a rub or anything? Come off it.

I stormed out and went straight round to Tracey's, where she was already on the phone. I knew she was speaking to the *blonde* who was tipping her off to get the story straight. Tracey denied this but then without hesitation gave me the same story, parrot fashion, as I had just been given by the *blonde*. I called her a filthy liar and went back.

Sarah was already there, and I called the pair of them names. They had their story straight by now though, and wouldn't budge an inch.

I stormed out intending never to return. Alone, I started to make a plan. I was finished with the *blonde* for sure. But first why not take advantage for myself of her wild nature? Why not sample a few of those delights? I must admit, I quite fancied a double headed blow job, and I thoroughly fancied both Tracey and the *blonde*. Who better to fulfill my dream?

I went back. I apologised for losing my temper. Said I was glad she had been brave enough to tell me the truth, and I forgave her as it was my own fault, for ignoring her in favour of computer chess. I would be OK now and pay her more attention. Could we try again? All lies.

She said yes. At that time I was still a wealthy man.

A few days later I put a proposition to her.

I promised I was OK about what she had done, and could forgive and forget. But I told her the idea of her indulging in this kind of sex was frustrating. I brought up the subject of the double headed blow job she and Wendy and given away for free.

Was it fair that some teenage kid who contributed nothing, should enjoy these pleasures and live to tell, when I, the backbone of her life would never experience the like? Was it fair?

She said she saw my point, but couldn't figure out how to accommodate me. There was no way her friends would go for a threesome with her steady boyfriend.

"What if we were all away on holiday with plenty of drugs and no tales told?"

"I could do that," she said. "As long as the other girl was a stranger." I went out and booked a week in Shagaluf. Then I went to Tracey's.

She was dubious about letting me in, but soon saw that I was not full of malice.

"Listen Tracey. You owe me. You lied to me when you had promised me the truth."

"Sorry," she said, shamefaced.

"Me and her have sorted things out and we're fine now. It's all forgotten. I know you're my friend and I came to apologise for earlier."

"OK. I'm sorry as well."

"How do you fancy coming on holiday? I've booked us a week in Ibiza and there's a spare seat on the plane."

"I can't afford it!"

I opened my wallet. "Let this be our secret Tracey, and don't forget. You owe me big-style."

Chapter 18

Shagaluf is full of nightclubs. As you know dear reader I don't do nightclubs well.

I was looking forward to some wild times there with my two girlies, both of who owed me big-style. But I knew they would want to be clubbing and I didn't want to be a wallflower. I wanted to be a party animal. The Shagaluf trip was two months away. I started to prepare.

The girls were planning a night out to see their favourite band in the next town. As usual I was offered the chance of accompanying them. Much to their surprise I accepted.

"But only if I can have some drugs."

When you first agree to take drugs with drug users they love you for it.

They can't wait to introduce you. I don't mean heroin which is something you either don't use or to which you are addicted. I mean speed, ecstasy, cocaine and cannabis. These are social drugs which can be used occasionally without becoming an addict.

You can get hooked: meaning that you enjoy the feeling so much you want more; but there are no physical pains or anxieties of withdrawal, as there are with smack. The *blonde* used them all, and when I asked for some the idea was such a novelty, that she readily agreed.

The "in" drug at the time was ecstasy. Me being prepared to take it added a whole new dimension to everyone's expectations of the evening.

I guess it's like showing someone your favourite movie or playing them a wonderful piece of music that you love but they haven't heard before. They can't wait to do it and to see your reaction.

She gave me a quarter of an e and waited for the result with sure knowledge of the fun to come.

There was no result. None at all.

I sloped off to the nightclub toilets with the surprisingly small piece of pill in my pocket. I locked myself in a cubicle, took it out and examined it carefully. How bad could a little piece of stuff like this be? I thought carefully: I had heard of people dying from a single dose of ecstasy. None of the girls or their friends had died though so why should I? I thought deeper.

A few years before, I had never seen an ecstasy tablet. Then I had witnessed their arrival on the streets we lived in. Now they were so common they were literally peddled door-to-door. A few more years and my son would be out on these streets being tempted by them; I needed to know what they did.

I swallowed it quickly and returned to the main room where all eyes were watching the toilet door I came out of.

It did nothing. But all night the girls were coming up to me asking me how I felt, had it kicked in yet? And the attention was wonderful.

At last I was one of the crowd. They couldn't believe it when I told them I was unaffected, but when I went home with the *blonde* we made wonderful love. If this is what it does, I thought, no problem trying it again. And a week later I did.

This time there was no hesitation. The fear of immediate death had been dispelled by reading up "the facts" on the internet: The active ingredient of the pill is MDMA, a substance devised by scientists in the fifties and prescribed to couples with relationship problems. It has no lethal qualities; a few years before, a rogue dealer had unknowingly cut the pure pills with rat poison, accidentally creating a deadly mixture which claimed a handful of victims before the error was known. This had accounted for some accidental deaths.

Other ecstasy related deaths had occurred where users had become so high they danced too long, and had forgotten to take in fluids; they died of dehydration. To avoid that problem drink plenty of water; but not too much in case the brain tissue absorbs it and you die of that.

I was sure the pills I had were OK as they were the same type as the *blonde* was using every week, and I knew how to drink water. I was safe. I popped the half a pill and waited. Again, nothing.

Except; there he was, in a new body, standing on the edge of the dance floor, watching the beautiful dancers. Beautiful dancers, dancing beautifully. And every one of them looking and smiling in his direction. Something gently brushed his back. Sensation shivered through him. Ecstasy!

I turned in alarm to see a gorgeous young woman look longingly into my face, as she eased past toward the dancers. He looked longingly back and moved towards her.

Suddenly I felt guilty. Shit! Had the blonde seen me eyeing up these girls?

Apprehensively I looked around, expecting the worst and to be going home alone.

The *blonde* and her three stunning mates were standing yards away laughing wildly. I made a helpless gesture. One came over, took me by the hand and leading me carefully back to the group. They clustered around me cooing. I was a Sultan with his harem.

"Come on babe, you stand over here with us where you'll be safe. Are you all right?"

And I was all right. Better than all right. I was buzzing. Not only was I now enjoying the nightclub. I was being allowed to!

When we got home the sex wasn't spectacular. I wanted it to be. So did she. But the mouth was dry for kissing and the erection was elusive.

Sleep was impossible except for an hour or so at dawn, but who needs sleep when waking dreams are better? We lay and cuddled and talked for hours. And in the morning: No hangover.

This is a better drug by far than alcohol I thought. And a lot cheaper!

An ecstasy tablet can cost you just two quid. With it you can stay out in the clubs till six in the morning without feeling one bit drained. And after only a few hours sleep you wake up still having that lovely feeling that everything's all right. And suddenly we had plenty to talk about, something in common. What a giggle for everyone!

The following weekend he I dropped another e. A full one.

This time the effect was less spectacular and wore off before the night was over so I dropped a second pill.

The pleasant anticipation was enough to get me through the time it took till it kicked in. Twenty minutes...half an hour... nothing, and then, before you knew it you were floating lighter than air. You would walk across the room past smiling people all welcoming and acknowledging you, and then your friends would walk over grinning, because they could see from the silly look on your face that you were high. That's how it was. It felt great.

Of course, as everybody knows, the great feeling gets less extreme with each and every usage. But you never stop hoping for a repeat of that first experience. And you never find it. It's still a good feeling but no time like the first.

The rest of the gang were taking other stuff besides ecstasy from time to time, and having crossed that line it wasn't hard for me to cross others. One night, after the clubs had closed, high on ecstasy and alcohol, I tried cocaine.

The *blonde* and her friends were less enthusiastic about this than they had been about passing me the odd pill. Naively I believed that this was concern for my welfare. I later realised that coke is a greedy drug that people don't like to share

For one thing it's expensive. Fifty pounds for about a teaspoonful of something like coarse white talc.

A fifty quid bag will thrill a moderate user for a whole night, but once you get a taste for it you want more.

When it runs out you search the carpets for dropped crumbs. No matter how much you've got of it, you use it till it runs out, and then you still want more.

You can go without sleep for three or four days and do hundreds of pounds worth of blow, if you can pay for it. It becomes more important than the mortgage, and while you're high you don't worry about building up arrears. You just keep on snorting, until your nose is blocked by the baking powder the local dealers mix into it to up their profits.

My first sniff wasn't like that though. It had hardly any effect at all and I decided I could do without it. I took my second sniff in Shagaluf.

Publisher's Afterword

So we have reached the higher heights of Rock & Roll and you still want more? I can't say as I blame you. When I first began working with Paul in 2012, he was submitting his memoir to a UK publishing contest and I asked if I could have a look. What I found was a juicy narrative filled with juicier dialogue locked in huge blocks of text. I told Paul no editor would get past the first few pages with those insurmountable blocks of tightly packed text and offered to attempt an edit/format with what I believed were my adequate skills only to stall midway thru the process over his thick Doncaster dialect.

We had a falling out over a change which I wrongly suggested and I set the manuscript aside for over a year as other life circumstances took over both of our ongoing stories. In late 2013, I reconnected with Paul, told him that his manuscript was perfect, but that I simply did not have what I felt was the necessary skill level to edit much further without mangling his memoir. I offered to find Paul a UK editor and had two suitable candidates that Paul desperately bedeviled and drove away and Paul and I had another falling out. This was likely mid 2014.

Life & circumstance brought Paul & I back together in mid 2015, and Paul asked me if I would act as an agent to find a publisher for his memoir. I agreed and formulated a strategy. I had completed nearly half of the editing and formatting so I put together promotional copies with a cover picture I designed and renamed his memoir "Sex, Droogs, Madness: Now But Madness Left" and with the help of my junior partner as agent, we strategically landed 9 copies of his promo on editor's desks via certified mail with a legal disclaimer that the materials were the exclusive promotional property of Burnt Hamster Publishing.

In the first round of promo mailings, of which only 19 copies were ever printed, we landed on 5 desks and received 1 rejection. I still have that letter in Paul's archive and it was one of the most encouraging and sincere rejection letters I have seen. We waited.

No further copies were returned, but neither did any of the remaining 4 editors reply.

In early 2016, I formulated a new plan to get the promo published using the emerging technology of crypto currency as a means of drawing enough sales to get a major publisher to bite and make an offer on Paul's memoir. We sent another round of promos and informed editors that we would be moving forward as soon as possible with a serialization of the memoir funded by cryptocurrency. 4 of those promo copies landed on editor's desks and again we waited as I began to learn the ins and outs of how to fund a project via cryptocurrency (which results you have just read, yes, it took me this long to fund the project.) Harper Collins was the only publisher in the second round to return the promo with a form letter stating they were returning the promo as the editor whose desk it landed on was no longer in their employ, deliberately misspelling "Burnt Hampster Publishing" both on the letter and in fancy handwriting on the cover of the envelope. So Paul's manuscript is still circulating 7 copies only Lord knows where at this point.

Nevertheless, we received no offers of a publishing contract and are now moving forward with serialization of Paul's memoir and you have finished Part I. So how does the memoir end in the depths and dregs of madness Paul into which Paul had descended? Well, like me, you are getting glimpses of that life in this release as I honestly did not want to continue mangling the manuscript with my primitive American editing capabilities and we are still hoping that sales of Part I will get Paul the contract he so richly deserves so I can enjoy the rest of his memoir edited by the hands of an editor who will do it the justice I feel I cannot. Stay tuned.

Agnew Pickens
July 12 2018